Designs for Wood

Designs for Wood

How to Plan and Create Your Own Furniture

Alonzo W. P. Kettless

Charles Scribner's Sons   New York

Copyright © 1978, 1975 Alonzo W. P. Kettless

Library of Congress Cataloging in Publication Data

Kettless, Alonzo William Percy.
  Designs for wood.

  1. Furniture design.   2. Furniture making.
Cabinet-work   I.   Title.
TT196.K47 1978   684.1'042   77-87177
ISBN 0-684-15541-9

1 3 5 7 9 11 13 15 17 19 Q/C 20 18 16 14 12 10 8 6 4 2

Printed in the United States of America

Contents

Conversion Tables

Imperial inches	Metric millimetres	Imperial inches	Metric millimetres	Metric millimetres	Imperial inches	Metric millimetres	Imperial inches
$\frac{1}{32}$	0·8	1	25·4	1	0·039	80	3·148
$\frac{1}{16}$	1·6	2	50·8	2	0·078	90	3·542
$\frac{1}{8}$	3·2	3	76·2	3	0·118	100	3·936
$\frac{3}{16}$	4·8	4	101·4	4	0·157	150	5·904
$\frac{1}{4}$	6·4	5	127·0	5	0·196	200	7·872
$\frac{5}{16}$	7·9	6	152·4	6	0·236	300	11·808
$\frac{3}{8}$	9·5	7	177·5	7	0·275	400	15·744
$\frac{7}{16}$	11·1	8	203·2	8	0·314	500	19·680
$\frac{1}{2}$	12·7	9	228·6	9	0·354	600	23·616
$\frac{9}{16}$	14·3	10	254·0	10	0·393	700	27·552
$\frac{5}{8}$	15·9	11	279·5	20	0·787	800	31·488
$\frac{11}{16}$	17·5	12	304·8	30	1·181	900	35·424
$\frac{3}{4}$	19·1	18	457·2	40	1·574	1,000	39·360
$\frac{13}{16}$	20·6	24	609·6	50	1·968		
$\frac{7}{8}$	22·2	36	914·4	60	2·362		
$\frac{15}{16}$	23·8			70	2·755		

Acknowledgements

The author and publisher would like to thank the following firms for kindly supplying photographs: Heal and Son Ltd., Hille International Ltd., John Makepeace, Gordon Russell Ltd., Archie Shine Ltd.

Line artwork drawn from author's originals by Cartographic Enterprises.

The author would like to thank Dr. Smith, Principal of Shoreditch College, for permission to use photographs of work produced by students of Shoreditch College;

his colleague Jim Fowles, principal lecturer and head of the woodwork department of Shoreditch College, for reading the manuscript;

Laurence Gall of Lowestoft for his skill and patience in taking many of the photographs;

his wife, Rose-Mary, for all her help and encouragement and for typing this manuscript.

Introduction

The designer-craftsman needs a good working knowledge of the various techniques of woodworking and allied crafts. To obtain the status of a professional craftsman a lengthy period of training covering both the practical and theoretical aspects is necessary. As well as knowing his material and techniques he must understand practical geometry, be capable of preparing rods and setting-out for machine and hand work and also appreciate the qualities of good design.

This book has been written in the hope that it will encourage apprentices, students, teachers and all woodwork enthusiasts to widen their horizons in craft and to take full advantage of the opportunities to practise good design.

Working with wood, in the true sense of craftsmanship, has a satisfaction seldom found in other materials.

Alonzo W. P. Kettless

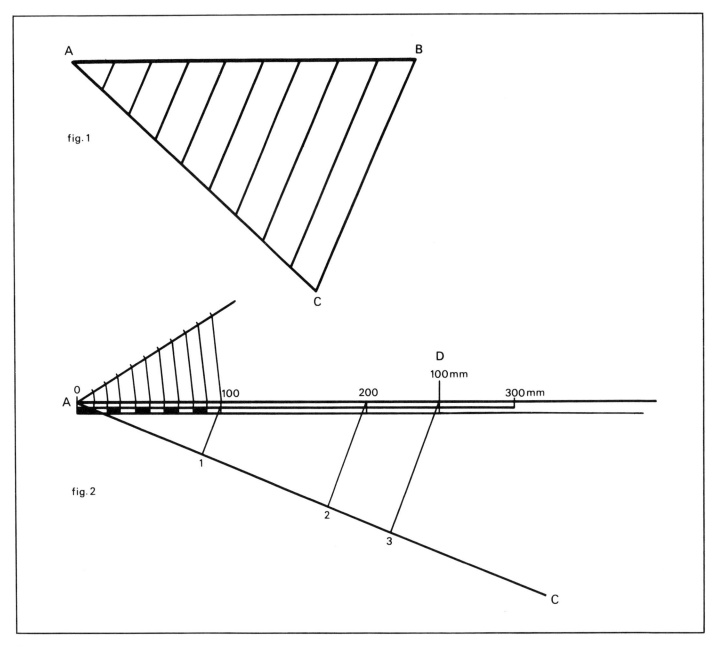

fig. 1

fig. 2

Craft geometry and setting-out

A sound knowledge of plane and solid geometry is one of the essential qualifications of a craftsman and is invaluable in the preparation of drawings, and in the accurate setting-out of work.

The range of problems given in this section is by no means comprehensive, but is, it is hoped, wide enough in its scope to enable the reader to become familiar with the practical applications of geometry.

Scales
When developing and producing drawings for industry, the designer must select the most convenient scale or representative fraction. For obvious reasons design drawings as required for the majority of the woodworking trades are usually made smaller than the objects they represent. For clarity, any special features of a design, for example, mouldings, handles, rail or stile sections, unusual joints, etc., are drawn out full-size.

Generally a scale should actually appear on the drawing. Metric scales are usually specified as 1:1 full-size, 1:2 half-size, 1:5, 1:10, 1:20, 1:50, 1:100, etc. The perusal of a designer's metric scale rule will make this quite obvious.

Scale rules showing feet and inches are generally available in 1:1 full-size, 1:2 half-size, 1:4 (3in − 1ft), 1:8 (1½in − 1ft), 1:16 (¾in − 1ft), etc. Often, scales to suit specific purposes, which are not readily available or convenient on scale rules, need to be constructed. Given the representative fraction these special scales are easily made with the aid of simple geometry, as described in Fig. 1 and 2.

The drawing in Fig. 1 explains a useful and practical geometrical method of dividing a line into a number of equal parts.

Division of lines
To divide a given line AB into any number of equal parts − say nine − draw a line AC at any convenient angle and mark off with compasses or ruler, the number of equal spaces required, in this case, nine. Join the last division C with B, and draw lines from all other points parallel to CB until they meet AB, which will be equally divided into nine spaces as required.

To construct a metric scale of say 1:2.5, representative fraction $\frac{2}{5}$ or 100mm represents 250mm (see Fig. 2). Draw a line of indefinite length from A and mark off D, 100mm. This will actually represent 250mm. Now applying proportional division to fix the units, draw a line AC of indefinite length and at any convenient angle, and mark off two equal spaces and one half of a space as shown at 1, 2, 3. Join 3 with D (100mm) and make 1 and 2 parallel with this line. This gives accurate proportional division, and the scale may be completed by numbering as shown 0, 100, 200, 300mm, etc.

The left-hand division can be further divided as shown into ten to represent divisions of 10mm in scale.

This technique of division applies when the dimensions are stated in metrics, as here, or in inches. It works the same either way.

Bisecting of angles

The accurate bisecting of an angle is a necessity when mitreing. The bisectors of some angles such as 90° and 60° are obvious, and are simply marked out with the use of set squares. There are other angles which require either the use of the protractor, or they are bisected by means of geometrical construction, such as the mitreing of mouldings for glazing bars, shaped work based on polygons, spandrils for staircase work, etc.

To bisect a given angle ABC see Fig. 1. With B as centre and any radius draw the arc DE. With D and E as centres draw arcs of equal radii intersecting at F. FB will bisect the angle ABC.
Fig. 2 shows mouldings intersecting at 75° and 110° respectively; it will be noticed that the overall angle is bisected.
Fig. 3 shows one corner of a barred door and the method of bisecting the various angles for correct mitreing of intersecting members.

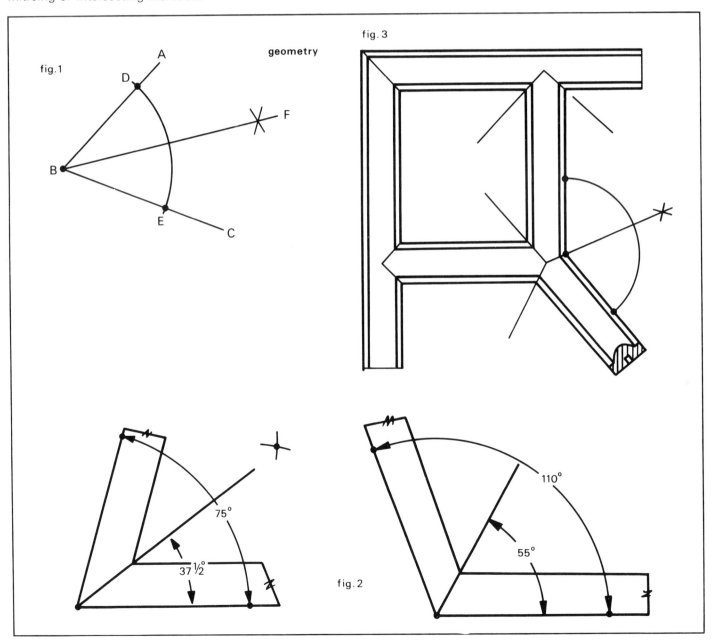

fig. 1

geometry

fig. 3

fig. 2

Polygons

A polygon is a plane rectilineal figure, bounded by more than four sides. When all the sides are equal and all the angles are equal, the figure is known as a regular polygon. Regular polygons are named in relation with the number of sides and angles contained in the figure, for example, a pentagon has five equal sides, a hexagon six, a heptagon seven (shown in Fig. 1), an octagon eight, a nonogon nine, etc.

To construct a regular pentagon on a given line, Fig. 2. Let AB be the given side. Extend the line to C and using A as centre describe a semi-circle CB. Divide the semi-circle into five equal parts by means of dividers and join A to 2. The second division 2 must always be used to determine the second line or first interior angle of the polygon.

Bisect AB and A2 and from the intersection O describe the circle touching the points BA2. The points DE can be obtained by stepping off distances equal to AB or A2. Complete the figure by joining all the points. This method applies to any regular polygon constructed on a given line.

Second Method, Fig. 3

Given side AB set off at A, angles of 45° and 60° to intersect the bisector of AB at points 4 and 6, 4 would be the centre of a circle passing through AB which would exactly circumscribe a square. Similarly 6 would be the centre of a circle circumscribing a hexagon. It follows that to find the centre for constructing a pentagon, bisect 4–6 as shown at 5. By marking off spaces equal to 4–5 the points 7 8 9 10 etc. can be marked off thus giving centres for circles circumscribing polygons with a similar number of sides.

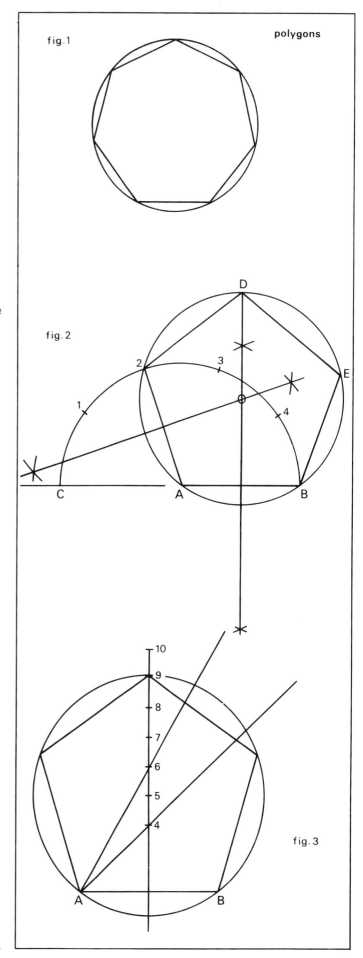

fig.1

polygons

fig.2

fig.3

11

To construct a regular polygon within a given circle, Fig. 4. Let AB be the diameter of the given circle in which a regular heptagon has to be constructed. Divide the diameter into seven equal parts by construction and number as shown. With A and B as centres and AB the radius, describe arcs meeting in C. From C through the second division draw the line CD, then BD is one side of the polygon. Complete by stepping off BD round the circle. This is an approximate method and is generally suitable for most practical purposes.

To construct a hexagon, Fig. 5, given the distance across two parallel sides as 40mm (1½in). Draw a circle of 20mm (¾in) radius. Draw parallel tangents AB and CD. With the 60° set square draw tangents as shown to complete the hexagon.

To inscribe an octagon, Fig. 6, in a square ABCD, draw the diagonals intersecting in O. With radius BO describe arcs with ABC and D as centres, and complete the octagon as shown.

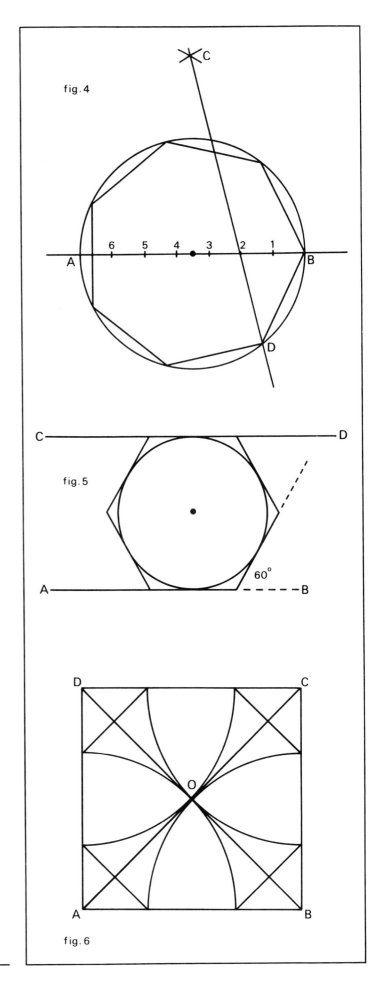

fig. 4

fig. 5

fig. 6

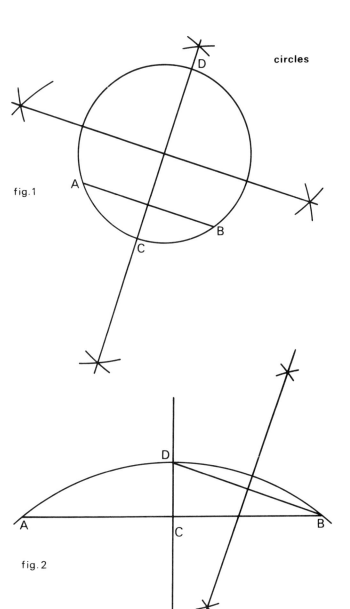

fig.1

fig.2

fig.3

Circles

To find the centre of a circle. Draw any chord AB and bisect it by a perpendicular CD, which is the diameter of the circle. Bisect CD to obtain the centre of the circle. See Fig. 1.

To mark out a segmented arch or arc, Fig. 2. With the span AB and rise CD being given, bisect the line DB and continue to meet the line DC produced, intersecting at P, giving the centre from which the segment can be drawn.

Fig. 3 shows a method of determining points on segmented curves of given span and rise when the centre is inaccessible. Draw the line AE at right angles to AD. ED is parallel to AB. Divide ED into, say, 5 equal parts, 1 – 4. Divide AC into the same number of equal parts, a – d. Join 1a, 2b, etc. Make AF perpendicular to AB and divide into the same number of equal parts as AC and ED. Draw radials from D to klm and n, giving intersections as points on the curve.

Fig. 4 shows how a thin batten and pins can be used when marking out shaped work.

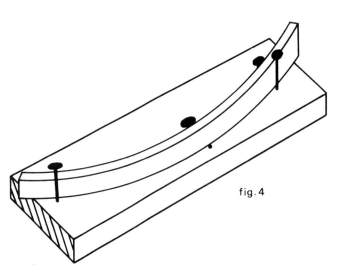

fig.4

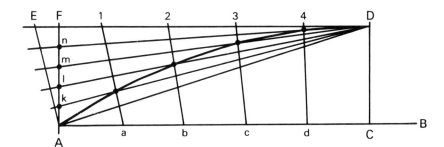

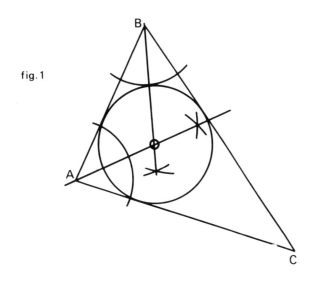

fig. 1

To draw an inscribed circle to a given triangle, Fig. 1. Bisect any two of the angles as ABC and BAC. The point O where these bisecting lines intersect is the centre of the required circle. With O as centre and radius equal to the perpendicular distance to any side of the triangle draw the circle.

To draw a circumscribing circle to a given triangle ABC Fig. 1A. Bisect any two sides of the triangle by lines at right angles to them. The intersecting lines at O will give the centre.

Setting out a trefoil

In the given circle, Fig. 2, draw in vertical diameter AB and draw tangent AC. Make a second diameter CD at 60° with the first. Bisect the angle ACD and draw in the equilateral triangle EFG as shown, which gives the centres for the three circles. Fig. 3 shows a trefoil complete with cusps.

Fig. 4 shows the method of inscribing any number of equal circles within a given circle, each to touch two others and the circumference of the circle. To inscribe four circles, divide the circle into eight parts — for five circles divide the circle into ten parts.

At A draw a tangent to the circle to meet the extended diameter at point B and bisect the angle ABC. The intersection at D is the centre, and DA the radius of the circle in sector CEF. With C as centre and CD as radius, mark off the centre of the other three circles and complete the quatrefoil.

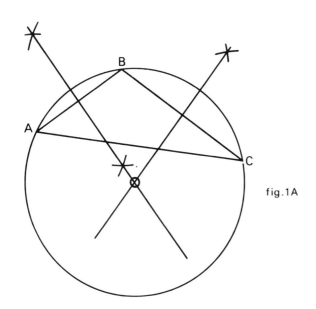

fig. 1A

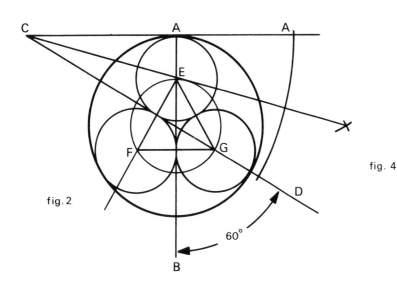

fig. 2

60°

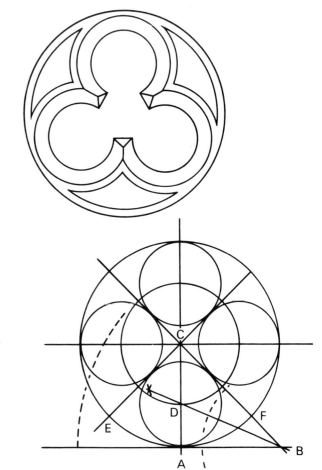

fig. 3

fig. 4

conic sections

fig. 1

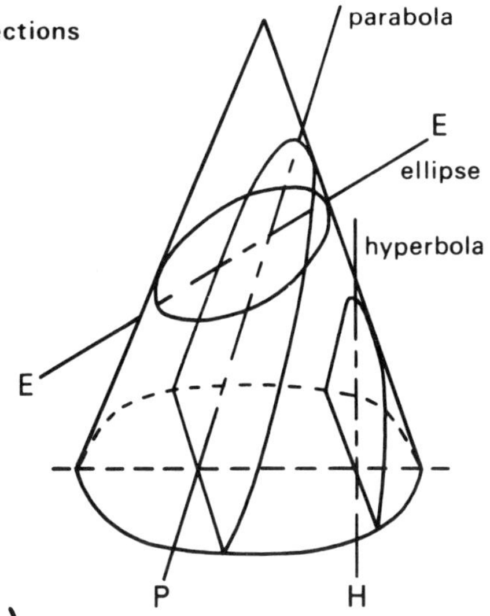

parabola

E

ellipse

hyperbola

E

P   H

fig. 2

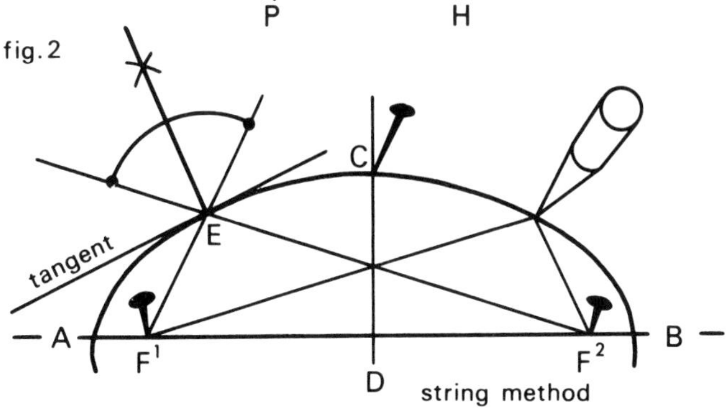

tangent

C

E

A   F¹   D   F²   B

string method

fig. 3

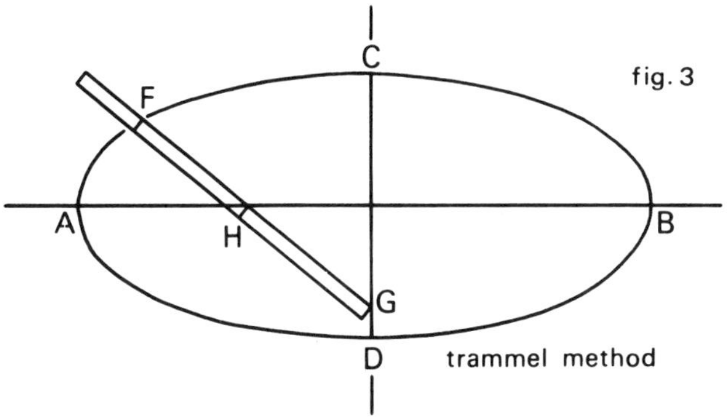

C

F

A   H   B

G

D   trammel method

fig. 4

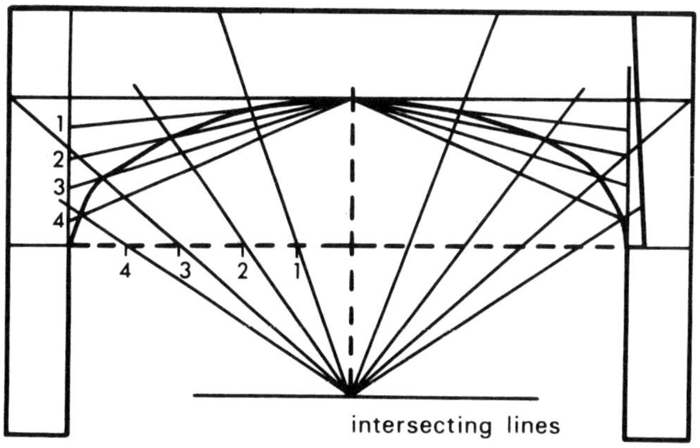

1
2
3
4

4   3   2   1

intersecting lines

Conic sections

The right cone is a solid generated by the revolution of a right-angled triangle about one of its sides forming the right-angle.

Conic Sections: If the cone is cut by a plane parallel to its base, the section produced will be a circle, and if inclined to the base as EE (Fig. 1), it produces an ellipse. When the cone is cut parallel to a side it produces a parabola and if cut parallel to its axis a hyperbola. These planes are shown diagramatically in Fig. 1. Conic sections are frequently used when designing buildings, architectural mouldings and in the joinery and furniture industries.

The ellipse

The ellipse may be defined as the locus or path of a point moving so that the sum of its distances from two fixed points is constant. The two fixed points are known as foci. The distance of any point on the curve to a focus is known as a focal distance. The sum of the focal distances is equal to the major axis.

String method: Given the major axis AB and semi-minor axis CD respectively of an ellipse to draw the curve using the String Method, Fig. 2. Using the information given in the above definition, take AD or BD as radius equal to half the major axis, and with C as centre describe arcs giving F^1 and F^2 as the foci of the curve, and by definition C is a point on the curve, since the focal distances F^1C and F^2C are by construction together equal to the major axis. Having found by construction points F^1C and F^2C and C, drive in pins as indicated in Fig. 2, pass a thread round the pins and secure. Remove pin at C and insert pencil and, keeping the thread taut, draw ellipse as shown.

Tangents and normals: Another property of the ellipse is that a normal to the curve bisects the angle between the lines forming the focal distance from any given point. Point E, Fig. 2, on the ellipse shows the focal lines bisected, thus giving the normal. A tangent is drawn at right angles to the normal.

Trammel method: Fig. 3 shows the trammel method for describing ellipses. Let AB and CD be the axes. The trammel can be made of paper or cardboard — normal drawing office practice — or for workshop use, of wood. Mark out on the trammel as follows: FG is made equal to half the major axis, and FH equal to half the minor axis. To mark out the ellipse, move the trammel around, keeping H and G on the respective axis lines, and a pencil point on F; this will give the path or locus of an ellipse.

Intersecting lines: Fig. 4 shows the method of describing an ellipse by means of intersecting lines, as could be applied when setting-out the top rail of an elliptical-headed door or framing. First draw the major and minor axis, which will give the span and rise to the elliptical curve. Then divide up the lines as shown into any number of equal parts, in this case five. Draw the intersecting lines through the divisions thus obtained, Fig. 4 shows this clearly. The ellipse is drawn in freehand

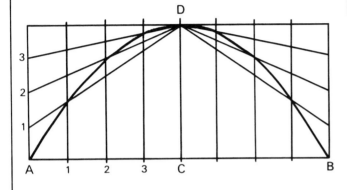

fig. 5

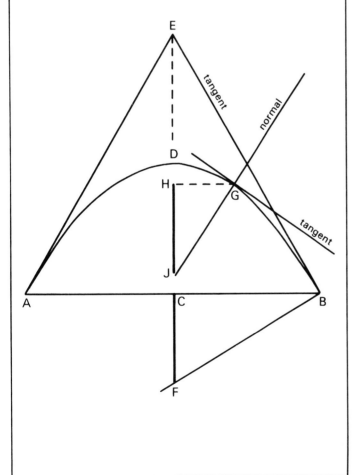

fig. 6

through the points of intersections as shown in the diagram.

The parabola

To draw a parabola, Fig. 5, by means of intersecting points having given the span AB and rise CD. Complete the enclosing rectangle and make any convenient number of divisions as shown at 1, 2 and 3; the corresponding intersections give points on the curve.

Fig. 6 shows how to determine a normal and a tangent to a parabola from any given point on the curve. Make DE equal to CD then EB will be a tangent to the curve at B. Draw BF at right angles to EB cutting the axis line in F then FC is the sub-normal which is constant.

In the construction of elliptical or parabolic wood arches or shaped framing, etc., it is essential that all joint lines should be on a normal to the curve and properly drawn. To find a tangent and a normal at point G or elsewhere on the curve, draw line GH, make HJ equal to the sub-normal CF. Join JG and produce as shown; this gives a normal to the curve. A line at right angles to JG through point G gives the tangent.

Mouldings

Fig. 1–10 cover a range of classical mouldings as used in Greek and Roman architecture.

All mouldings used in architecture and woodwork are based on these examples. Small mouldings are often grouped together to form larger mouldings such as those required for making up cornices and plinths, etc. (see Fig. 11, page 18). It is considered necessary — as part of his training — for the designer-craftsman to make a particular study of these various mouldings with relation to their properties and the difference between the Grecian and Roman types.

Grecian mouldings are more refined and are principally based on elliptical and parabolic curves, and are usually drawn in free-hand. Roman mouldings are bolder and these are mainly constructed of quadrants. The mouldings we use today have been developed or modified from these classical shapes and the profiles of many of them are still in use.

Light and shade: The lines of light and shade produced by mouldings give character to parts of buildings, furniture, etc., by accentuating their chief features. Mouldings are decorative rather than constructional and a careful study of their profiles, proportions and the position they occupy in relation to the eye is well worth while (see Fig. 11, page 18).

Panel and other mouldings: Sections showing a wide range of panel mouldings and mouldings suitable for table tops and carcase edge treatments, etc., are given on page 18.

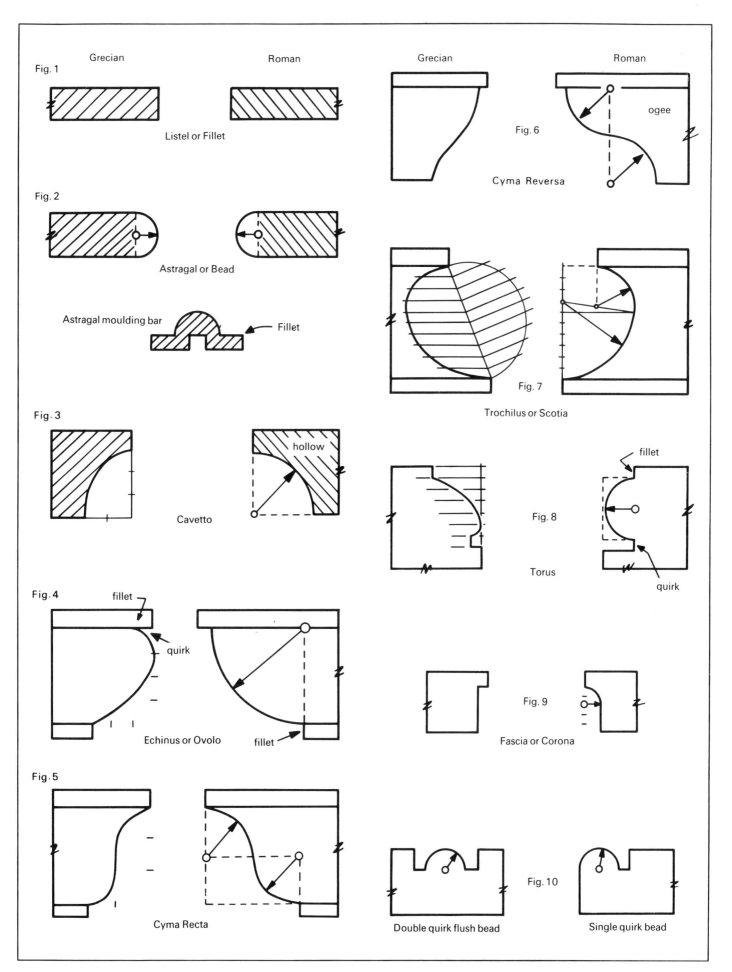

Fig. 1   Grecian   Roman

Listel or Fillet

Fig. 2

Astragal or Bead

Astragal moulding bar — Fillet

Fig. 3

hollow

Cavetto

Fig. 4

fillet

quirk

Echinus or Ovolo   fillet

Fig. 5

Cyma Recta

Grecian   Roman

Fig. 6   ogee

Cyma Reversa

Fig. 7

Trochilus or Scotia

fillet

Fig. 8

Torus   quirk

Fig. 9

Fascia or Corona

Fig. 10

Double quirk flush bead   Single quirk bead

17

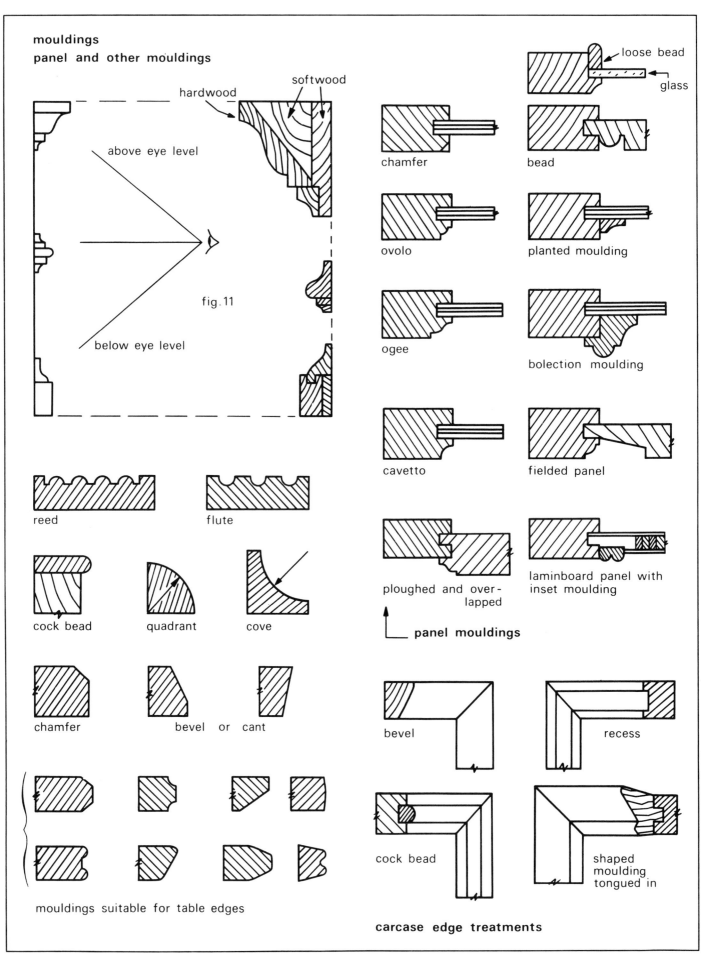

mouldings
panel and other mouldings

above eye level

below eye level

fig. 11

hardwood

softwood

reed

flute

cock bead

quadrant

cove

chamfer

bevel or cant

mouldings suitable for table edges

chamfer

ovolo

ogee

cavetto

ploughed and over-
lapped

loose bead

glass

bead

planted moulding

bolection moulding

fielded panel

laminboard panel with
inset moulding

panel mouldings

bevel

recess

cock bead

shaped
moulding
tongued in

carcase edge treatments

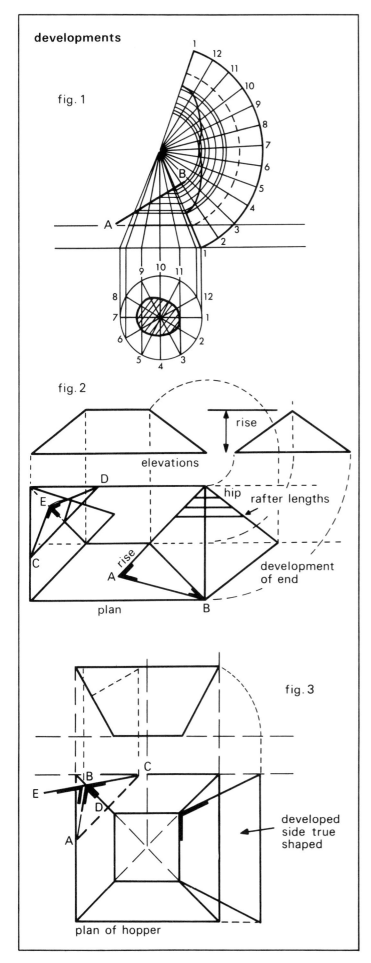

developments

fig. 1

fig. 2

elevations

rise

plan

hip

rafter lengths

rise

development
of end

fig. 3

developed
side true
shaped

plan of hopper

Developments

Given the plan and elevation, Fig. 1, of a right cone cut by an inclined plane AB, draw the development (the unfolding or laying flat the surface of an object).

Divide the plan into twelve equal parts, number as shown and draw vertical projectors from plan to meet base in elevation. Join these points with the apex as shown in Fig. 1. The radiating lines shown in plan and elevation of the cone represent imaginary lines resting on its surface; these are known as generators. With the apex as centre, and the true length of a generator as radius, draw an arc of indefinite length and mark off with dividers the points 1, 2, 3–12. 1, as shown in Fig. 1. This is an approximate development of the circumference of the base of the cone, and is considered satisfactory for most practical applications. From where the cut surface of the cone intersects the generators, project horizontally on to the true length of a generator as shown in elevation. With the aid of compasses transfer these lengths on to corresponding numbered generators. Draw a free-hand curve through these points to complete the development.

The drawing also shows the cone cut by a horizontal plane, and method for developing its surface. This is the usual method of developing material for conical lampshades.

Bevelled work, roof bevels and hoppers
Fig. 2 shows the plan and elevation of a hipped roof and the simple geometry involved when finding the lengths and bevels of hips and rafters, etc.

AB gives the length and bevels for hip rafters, while CED shows backing for hips and intersecting joint lines for framed roof lights. The drawings are self-explanatory.

Fig. 3 shows the plan and elevation of a hopper, and the geometry and bevels required for marking out the true shape of sides. The angle ABC gives the dihedral angle between the two inclined planes, and angle ABD is used when mitreing the sides.[1] The angle ABE is required when marking out for dovetails, and for making tongue and groove joints at the intersections.

Fig. 4, page 20, shows the plan and elevation of a triangular hopper, and method of finding (1) the dihedral angle between intersecting surfaces, (2) bevel for mitre edges, and (3) development of one side.

Make $X^1 Y^1$ parallel to AB and produce construction lines from AB as shown and mark off height of hopper $C^1 D^1$. Draw $C^1 C^2$. From any convenient point on C^1 E set out line EG at right angles to $C^1 C^2$. Imagine this line to represent a plane which is at right angles to $C^1 C^2$ and draw in EF. It will be apparent that this plane is triangular in shape and cuts the two edges at F^1 F as shown in plan.

---

[1]The hip backing CED in Fig. 2 is also the dihedral angle between two inclined planes.

Now imagine this triangular plane rotated about the line F¹ F until it is in a horizontal position, then G would move to G¹. Project G¹ down to line AB to obtain point H. Join H to F¹, and F to obtain angle between surfaces as shown. Bisect this angle to obtain bevels for mitres. KLMN gives the development – true shape – and bevels for the inside surface of one side.

Hemispherical dome
When covering domes or niches with wood or veneers, a double curvature is involved, and this presents certain problems.

Method 1: If the dome is to be cladded (covered) with narrow horizontal strips, it is necessary to develop each one as shown in Fig. 1. These developments are called *zones*.

Method 2: Imagine the dome cut into small segments – see Fig. 2 plan – then the outer developed surfaces would be known as *gores*.

The methods shown in Fig. 1 and 2 are approximate and sufficiently accurate for most practical purposes. It is obviously an advantage to keep the sections small and an allowance should be made for fitting.

Development of domical surfaces
Draw the plan and section outlines on XY Fig. 2 and 1. Divide the left-hand side of section (quadrant) into 6 equal parts, giving horizontal sections 0.1.–5.6. Draw vertical projectors from these points to the diameter in plan and number as before. From centre O draw the concentric plan circles of the 6 zones. If we imagine that the dome is enclosed in six cones the slant sides of the frustums being 01 1.2 2.3 3.4 4.5 5.6 then each of these slant sides are produced to meet the vertical line through the centre, two of which are shown, giving F and G as apices of the cones. With F as centre and F¹ F² as radii draw the semi-zones as shown.

Similarly from G as centre and radii G2 and G3 a second zone can be drawn. Repeat the procedure for the remaining zones. The stretch out for the zones can be seen in plan, the bottom edge of each zone gives the stretch out (correct dimension). Step off carefully this dimension and transfer to the appropriate developed zones.

For the development of a gore five divisions are taken as A B C D E 6 from elevation.

The number of gores depends on the size and nature of the work, and for this example eight are taken in half-plan. Projectors drawn from the points AB to E6 in elevation to the diameter in plan enable the concentric plan circles to be drawn.

To determine the approximate shapes for the gores, a series of vertical sections are drawn, and the plan Fig. 2 shows one half of the dome divided into the equivalent of eight parts. The method of stretch out and development of gores will be apparent from the drawings.

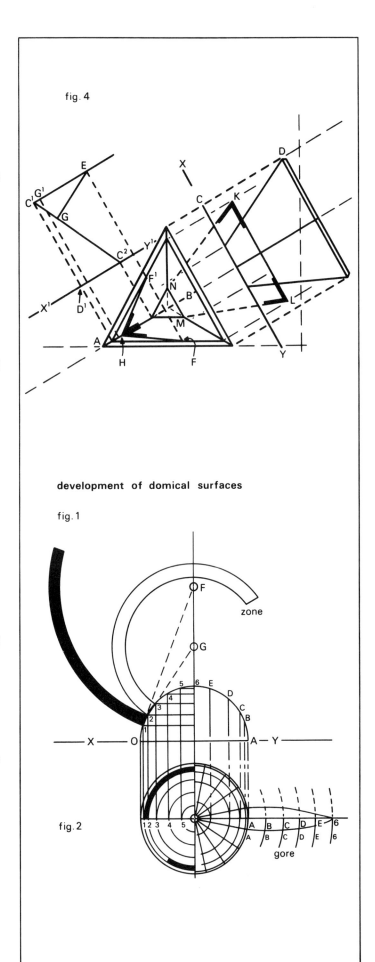

fig. 4

development of domical surfaces

fig. 1

zone

fig. 2

gore

Proportional reduction and enlargement of mouldings

The reduction and enlargement of mouldings is based upon one of the properties of the triangle.

An equilateral triangle with base line AB is divided into a given number of parts as shown in Fig. 1.

If datum lines are drawn from 1 2 3 and 4 to the apex C, then any horizontal line such as DD, EE, FF which they cut will be in the same ratio as the base line. Fig. 2 shows quite clearly that the shape of the triangle makes no difference to the ratio, but in practice either equilateral or right-angled triangles are used.

Reduction of mouldings

Fig. 3 shows in section a moulding ABC which it is necessary to reduce proportional to a new height given as HH. Applying the above geometrical principle of the triangle draw the section ABC of the moulding on XY line and extend vertical line AC to D. Project vertical lines from profile of moulding as shown at CY and with C as centre draw quadrants to cut line CD at 1–8.

Horizontal datum lines are also drawn from the profile, and cut line AC at a b c d e, etc. From a convenient distance X draw lines XA and XD. Given new height of moulding as HH then project horizontally to intersect line XA at A1, and draw vertical line $A^1 D^1$. Lines drawn from a b c d, 1 2 3 4 5 etc., to X will cut line $A^1 D^1$ in the same ratio as AD. With C^1 as centre the quadrant lines are drawn until they cut the line XY.

Draw in vertical and horizontal lines to give points of intersection for profile of moulding as shown in sketch.

It is obvious from a study of the drawings that to enlarge a given moulding it is necessary to draw the triangle XAD, and the new height AC which is extended to D. The profile of the moulding is easily completed.

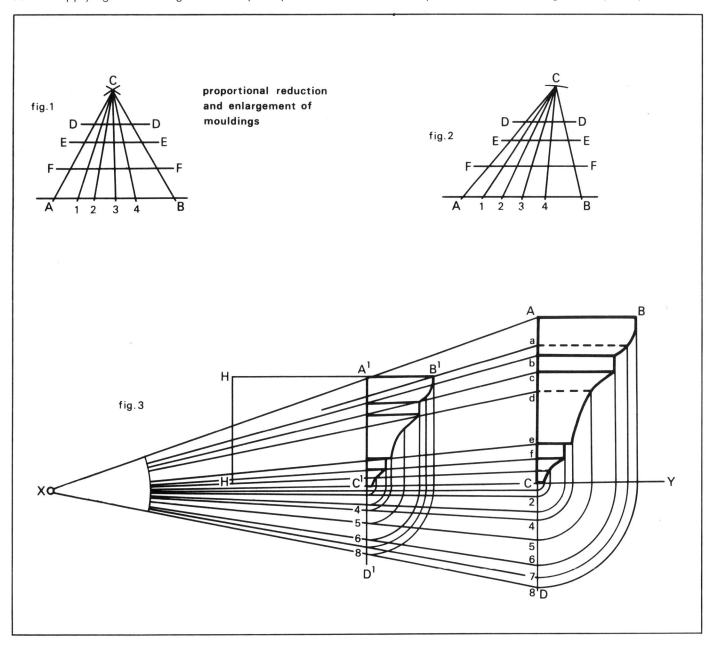

proportional reduction and enlargement of mouldings

fig.1

fig.2

fig.3

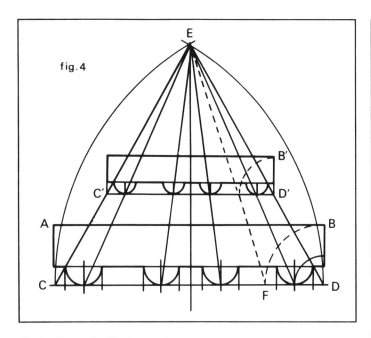

fig. 4

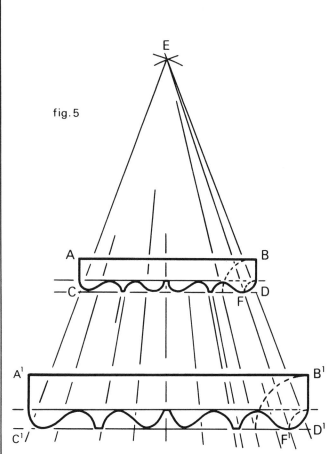

fig. 5

Reduction of pilaster section

A section of a pilaster ABCD which has to be reduced in size is given in Fig. 4.

First draw an equilateral triangle on base line CD and draw reference lines from the profile to the apex E. Draw C′D′ the required width of the new moulding. To find the thickness of pilaster, take D as centre and draw arc BF and join F with E. With D′ as centre construct arc to give D′B′, which is the proportional thickness of new moulding.

To enlarge a pilaster section

Draw a section of the pilaster ABCD as shown in Fig. 5, and construct the equilateral triangle, from centres C and D giving E as apex.

From E draw main reference lines cutting points on profile, extending sufficiently to cater for profile of enlarged moulding C^1D^1.

To find thickness and depth of moulding D^1B^1 construct arcs as shown, at D and B and F, and draw reference lines as shown. These cut the required section thus giving radius to complete thickness B^1D^1.

The method outlined above can also be applied to turned work, balusters, legs, etc.

Proportional reduction

Given a jamb architrave A, Fig. 6, or any other moulding which is required to intersect as a mitre with another moulding of less width.

First draw the given architrave A. The narrower moulding determines the mitre and the thickness remains constant. Projectors are drawn from convenient points on profile of given moulding A. The plotting of the new cross-section is apparent from the drawing.

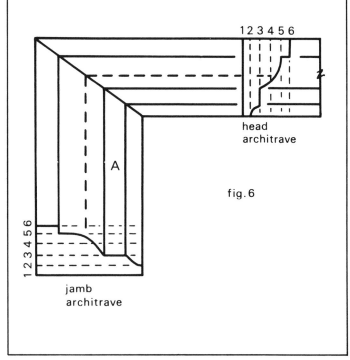

1 2 3 4 5 6

head architrave

fig. 6

A

1 2 3 4 5 6

jamb architrave

raking moulds

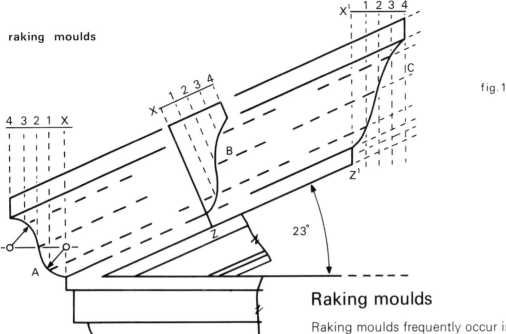

fig. 1

carved mouldings

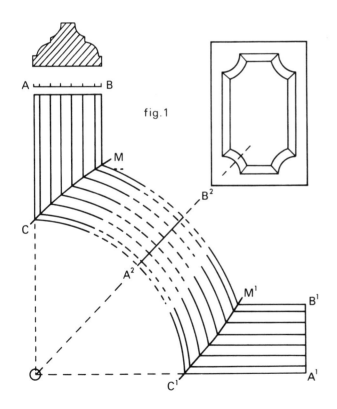

fig. 1

Raking moulds

Raking moulds frequently occur in architecture, particularly in relation to woodwork and masonry. The geometry involved in solving a practical problem is given in Fig. 1 above. This shows the details for a straight pitched stone or wood pediment. The Cyma Recta mould A is placed horizontally on one surface of a structure and is met by another mould B running at an inclination across an adjacent surface. The mould B is commonly termed a raking mould. The Cyma Recta mould A is taken as the given mould from which B and C are obtained.

For a closed pediment the mould B would be used on both sides and brought to a vertical mitre at the apex. To find profile of moulds B and C, erect projectors from convenient points on the profile of given mould A to cut horizontal line X4 and number 1–4 as shown. Draw line XZ at right angles to raking mould B, and line X4 as shown numbering as before. Draw projectors from 1–4 as shown. To find mould C draw line X^1Z^1 and repeat construction as before. Projectors drawn from given mould meet projectors from X^1–4 thus giving intersecting points for profile of moulds B and C.

Curved mouldings

The line diagram in Fig. 1 represents a large veneered panel decorated with a planted moulding as given in section AB. This is a good practical example of the use of loci as applied to curved mitres.

To obtain a true intersection at the mitre between the curved and straight mouldings shown in Fig. 1, it is necessary to find the loci as set out in Fig. 1.

Draw projectors from convenient points on profile of given moulding to intersect datum line AB as shown. Set off datum line A^1 B^1 and with centre O and radius taken from datum line A^2 B^2 complete construction, which will determine curved mitres CM and C^1M^1.

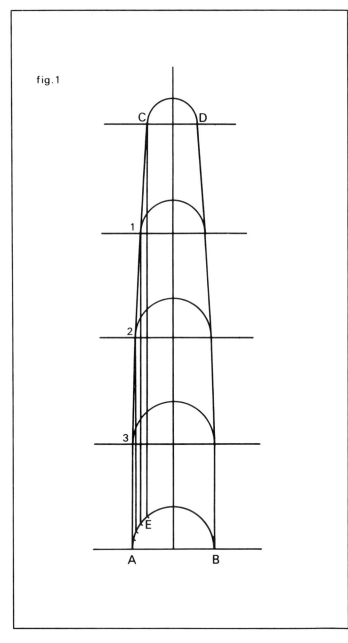

fig.1

Entasis of column

The sides of column if made perfectly straight and parallel would, when viewed from a distance, appear concave. This is an optical illusion and to obviate this apparent concavity the columns are usually made smaller at the top, and are given a convex swelling or curvature, see Fig. 1. It also gives the impression of stability to the supported fabric. This swelling or convexity of the sides is known as the *entasis*.

Let AB equal the base diameter, and CD the diameter of the top. Divide the height into four parts and drop a projector from C to E. Divide the arc AE into a similar number of parts, and erect projectors giving points 1 2 3. A fair curve drawn through the points C 1 2 3 A will give the entasis.

The entasis of a column does not always spring from the base line, but may commence 685mm (2ft 3in) above the base line.

Setting-out

The main qualifications of a setter-out are:
1 He should possess a thorough knowledge of his craft — including actual bench experience — and be well acquainted with all kinds of construction and workshop techniques.
2 He should have a good understanding of machine shop organisation and practice.
3 A sound knowledge of plain and solid geometry, coupled with drawing-office experience.

The setter-out: He is usually an experienced craftsman who is mainly engaged in extracting information from the designers' scale drawings and specifications and making full-size sections — usually horizontal and vertical — through the job and showing all details of construction and information necessary for the manufacture of the article. These sections are usually drawn out on strips of hardboard, plywood or on rolls of paper, and are known as *rods*.

The rods, when drawn out on hardboard or plywood, can easily be erased by covering the surface with a coat of white emulsion paint, and used again for a fresh job.

Hardboard is also suitable for setting-out full-size details of chairs, and jobs with special features from which patterns or templates are to be made.

When preparing rods for joinery for large public buildings, ship work, etc., the sections are usually drawn on rolls of paper, and all major dimensions are clearly stated. This precaution is necessary, as paper is liable to expand or contract with changing temperatures. All major dimensions must be checked when actually setting-out off the rod and on to the material.

Use of rods

Cutting lists (description and size of all parts needed to make the job) are prepared from the rods and sent to the mill, so that the material can be selected and prepared for setting-out. The prepared material is then conveyed to the setter-out, who selects the relevant pieces and locates them on the rod and marks out all joints and essential details so that the various parts can be machined and made ready for the craftsman to assemble. An example of setting-out is given on page 25, showing the height and width rods for a small cabinet and the method of setting-out for a one-off, hand or machine job. With the linenfold panel illustrated on page 35 is the working drawing showing horizontal and vertical sections and all the information necessary to make the panel.

The photograph on page 27 shows a portion of a gunstock door stile, with bedded bolection mouldings and fielded panels. An elevation of a similarly constructed door and the rods required for setting-out are shown on page 26. See Fig. 1, for method of setting-out on material.

The drawings on page 28 show the plan, elevations and enlarged details of a small semi-circular table with

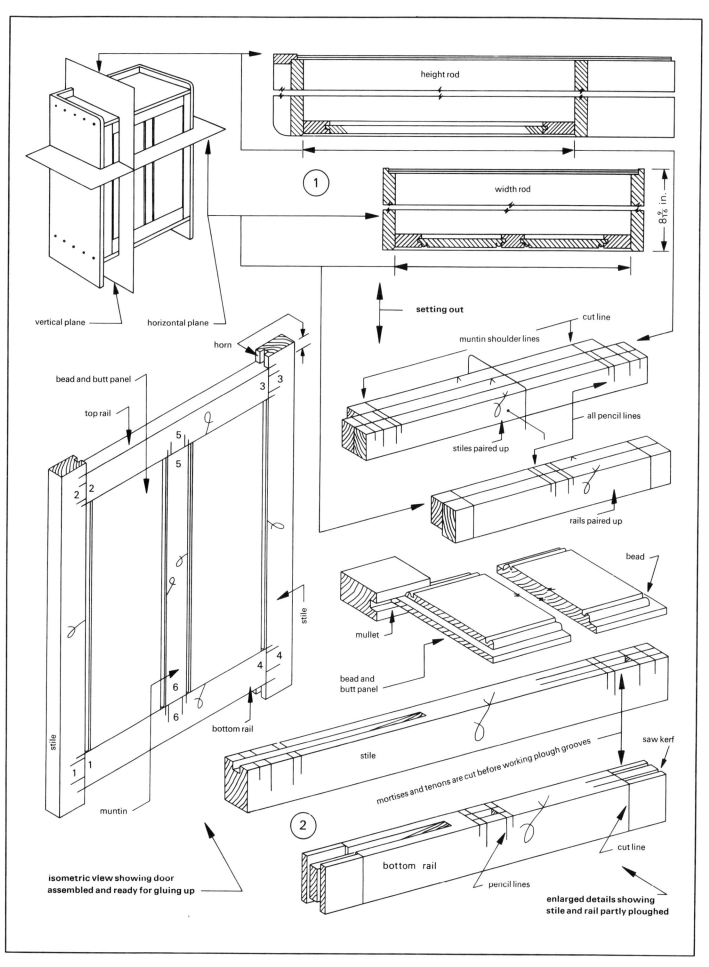

vertical plane

horizontal plane

① height rod

width rod

$8\frac{9}{16}$ in.

setting out

cut line

muntin shoulder lines

all pencil lines

stiles paired up

rails paired up

bead

mullet

bead and butt panel

stile

mortises and tenons are cut before working plough grooves

saw kerf

② stile

bottom rail

pencil lines

cut line

**enlarged details showing
stile and rail partly ploughed**

horn

bead and butt panel

top rail

stile

stile

muntin

bottom rail

**isometric view showing door
assembled and ready for gluing up**

25

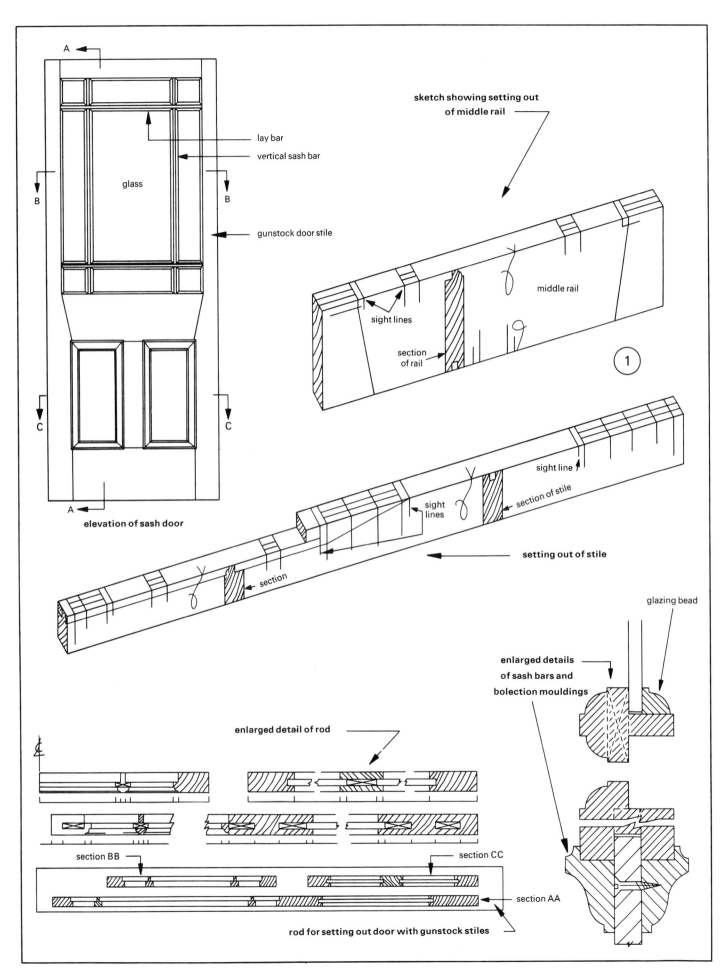

A

lay bar

vertical sash bar

glass

gunstock door stile

B   B

C   C

A

elevation of sash door

sketch showing setting out of middle rail

sight lines

section of rail

middle rail

①

sight line

sight lines

section of stile

section

setting out of stile

glazing bead

enlarged details of sash bars and bolection mouldings

enlarged detail of rod

₵

section BB

section CC

section AA

rod for setting out door with gunstock stiles

Semi-circular table in teak.

Portion of door with gunstock or diminished stile, bedded bolection moulding and fielded panels.

laminated rim. When making this table it would be advisable to draw the plan full-size, so that the necessary former for the laminated rim and setting-out could be accurately and efficiently executed. A photograph of the table is shown above.

The drawings on page 29 give joints and setting-out details for basic stool construction.

A rod for a linen chest is shown on page 29. Note the adjustable setting-out gauge used for drawing parallel lines. Details A and B show alternative construction and panel arrangements respectively. Shown on page 31 are the setting-out details of a hopper, and the explanation of the geometry involved is given on page 19.

A working drawing for a sideboard, giving vertical and horizontal sections, is shown on page 30.

There are numerous designs illustrated throughout this book giving constructional information and sectional details essential when preparing rods and setting-out.

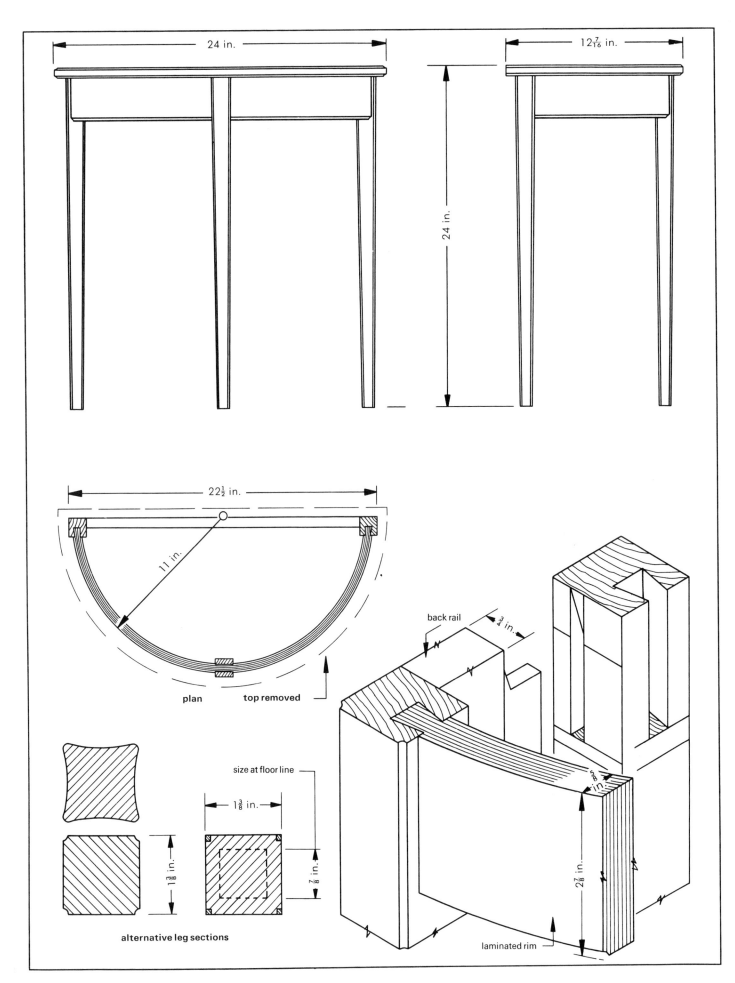

24 in.

$12\frac{7}{16}$ in.

24 in.

$22\frac{1}{2}$ in.

11 in.

plan   top removed

size at floor line

$1\frac{3}{8}$ in.

$1\frac{3}{8}$ in.

$\frac{7}{8}$ in.

alternative leg sections

back rail

$\frac{3}{4}$ in.

$2\frac{7}{8}$ in.

laminated rim

$\frac{7}{8}$ in.

28

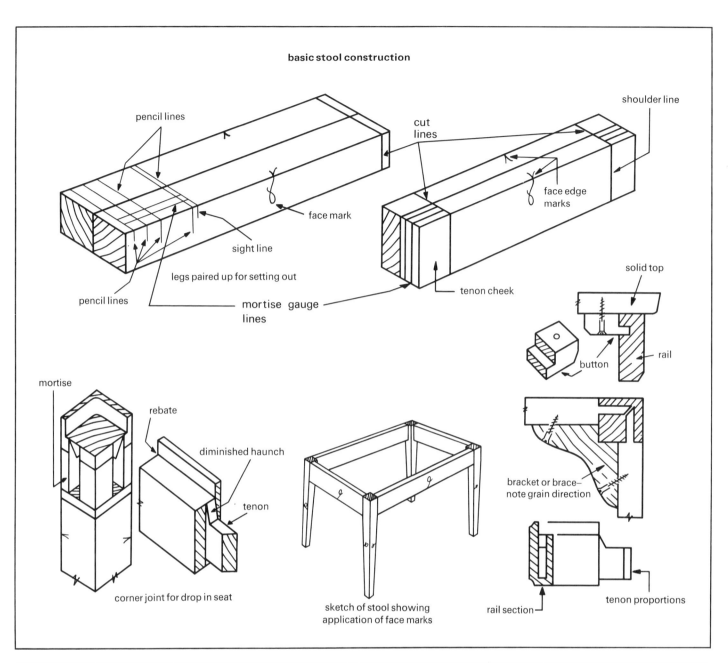

basic stool construction

pencil lines

cut lines

shoulder line

pencil lines

sight line

legs paired up for setting out

face mark

face edge marks

mortise gauge lines

tenon cheek

solid top

button

rail

mortise

rebate

diminished haunch

tenon

bracket or brace—note grain direction

corner joint for drop in seat

sketch of stool showing application of face marks

rail section

tenon proportions

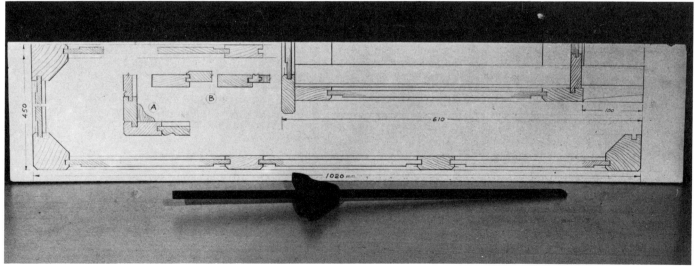

Rod for linen chest.
In the foreground can be seen an adjustable setting-out gauge.

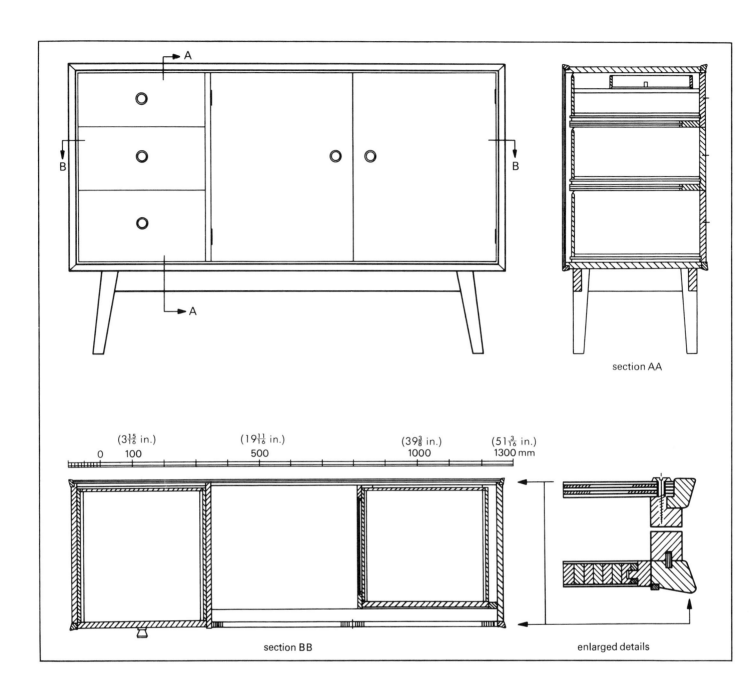

section AA

$(3\frac{15}{16}$ in.) $(19\frac{11}{16}$ in.) $(39\frac{3}{8}$ in.) $(51\frac{3}{16}$ in.)

0   100   500   1000   1300 mm

section BB

enlarged details

Setting-out for hopper.
Note large wood try-square and compasses in foreground.

Workshop-made tools and appliances

The following tools, illustrated on page 33, are usually made, rather than purchased, by the craftsman. They have been arranged for clarity into three main groups.

A For general bench work
B For setting-out
C For special work, such as veneering, inlaying, and short runs of mouldings for prototype jobs and work incorporating mitres

A General bench work

1 Winding strips: Used for testing work for wind or twist. The small insets, when made of bone or white plastic material, aid sighting. Useful as small straight edges.
2 Straight edge and squaring rod: For testing and marking out.
3 Bench hook
4 Wood, set and try square
5 Mitre template: When mouldings are stuck, i.e. worked in the solid, for doors, windows and frames, the mouldings are usually mitred or scribed. The template is made out of one piece of wood (any suitable hardwood) and the ends are cut and planed at 45°. The diagrams on page 57 show mitreing and scribing techniques.
6 Mitre template for stopped chamfers
7 Adjustable cramps with folding wedges

B Setting-out

8 Box square: The square is made out of one piece of hardwood. It is particularly useful for setting-out work where there would be no bearing surface for the stock of a normal try-square as is the case with material already moulded for doors and window sashes, etc.
9 Adjustable setting-out gauge: For use on the setting-out table, see page 29.
10 Try square
11 Large bevel
12 Compasses
13 Gauges for circular work
14 Centre square: Particularly useful for finding centres

when working with cylindrical material. Accurate setting-out and boring of holes are essential when making this square.
15 Dovetail template: 1–8 bevel for hardwood, 1–6 for softwood.

C Special work

16 Scratch stock: Most useful for scratching in grooves to receive inlays, strings and bandings. It is also used for making small runs of special mouldings which would not be economical to produce by machine, see page 34. It consists of two pieces of wood shaped and screwed together to form a stock which is held firmly against the edge or side of the job. Old scrapers make excellent material for cutters. The cutter is sharpened by filing across at right angles, thus enabling the scratch to be used on both the forward and backward movements. To make a groove to receive strings or bandings, cut and file the cutter to the exact width of the string. Try out on a small piece of wood and test for size. The string or banding should be finger tight.

17 Veneer hammer: A necessity when veneering by hand. It is used for pressing down the veneer and squeezing out the glue. It consists of a head shaped to form a comfortable grip for the hand, and a handle which is fixed to the head by wedging. The head is grooved to take the brass strip which should not be less than 2mm ($\frac{3}{32}$in) thick.
18 Shooting board
19 Mitre shooting board
20 Mitre sawing box
21 Mitre shooting block: See page 35.

dowels

steel piping

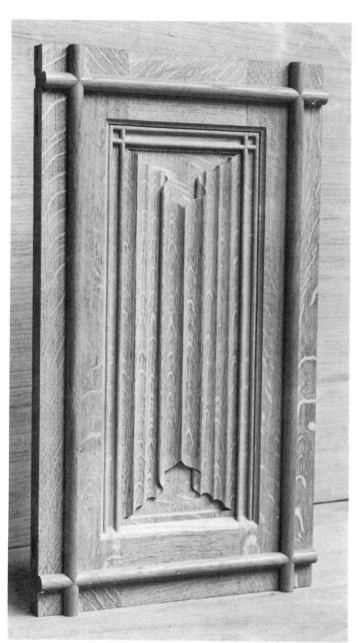

Linenfold panel

The photographs on pages 34 and 35 show a linenfold panel made by the author for the Worshipful Company of Carpenters 1958 Craft Competition.

The task set for this competition was a linenfold panel with shaped and recessed ends, the frame having a double reeded moulding worked on the solid, with solid worked stops at the bottom finishing on a bevelled edge and intersecting to corners finished as bishop's mitres. The job was required to be made by hand, and finished left from the tool.

The panel is contained within a case of sapele and incorporated in the lid is the author's colour-washed drawing, showing horizontal and vertical sections.

Two scratch stocks and various cutters are shown on page 34. In the foreground can be seen the cutters which the author made to work the mouldings for the frame. On the right are shown two files which were used for shaping the cutters.

Left:
Linenfold panel.

Below left:
Scratch stocks and moulding.

Below:
Mitre shooting block.

Metal fittings and cabinet brass work

Nails and screws

Nails

Many different types of nails are used in the woodworking industries. Nails are used for fixing or holding wood or other material together or where particular joints need strengthening. They are usually sold by weight. The furniture-maker has occasional use for a variety of nails which have small inconspicuous heads, such as panel and veneer pins and oval brads. These are mainly used for fixing mouldings, making mock-ups, jigs and prototypes, etc. A useful range of nails together with a description of their uses is shown on page 37.

A Lost-head wire nail: Used for carpentry and joinery, sizes 37mm–100mm (1½in–4in) in bright mild steel or galvanized.

B Oval wire nail: Also known as *Oval brad*. Used mainly for joinery, fixing mouldings and architraves, etc., sizes 12mm–150mm (½in–6in), finish bright mild steel or galvanized.

C French or wire nail: Used for carpentry and case making, sizes 12mm–150mm (½in–6in), finish bright mild steel or galvanized.

D Cut clasp nail: Used for carpentry, fixing rafters, skirting, picture rails, etc., sizes 19mm–200mm (¾in–8in), finish black iron.

E Cut floor brad: Used for carpentry, fixing floor boards, sizes 37mm–75mm (1½in–3in), finish black iron.

F Wire clout nail: Used for fixing roofing felt, canvas, etc., sizes 19mm–75mm (¾in–3in), finish bright mild steel or galvanized.

G Panel pins: Used for joinery and cabinet making, sizes 9mm–50mm (⅜in–2in), finish bright mild steel, brass and coppered.

H Veneer pins: Used for fixing small mouldings, veneers, etc., sizes 9mm–37mm (⅜in–1½in), finish bright mild steel.

J Cut tack: Used for upholstery, carpets, etc., sizes 6mm–32mm (¼in–1¼in), finish blued, black iron or copper.

K Sprig: Used for glazing, picture backs, etc., sizes 12mm–19mm (½in–¾in), finish black iron.

L Hardened fixing pin: Used for fixing to masonry, sizes 19mm–62mm (¾in–2½in).

M Screw nail: Used for fixing metal to wood, sizes 6mm–50mm (¼in–2in), finish bright steel plated.

N Hardboard pin: Used for fixing hardboard, popular sizes 19mm–25mm (¾in–1in), finish sherardized and coppered.

Screws

Screws have greater holding power than nails, create less shock when driving in and are easily removed and replaced. They are used for securing to wood, fittings such as hinges, locks, handles and bolts. They are also used for reinforcing light framework, fixing table tops, drawer runners, and knock-down furniture, etc. Screws are usually known by the type of head and the kind of metal from which they are made. Three main types, as shown in Fig. 1, are:

A Countersunk head;
B Round head;
C Raised head;
D A popular type of mirror screw is shown.

The Phillips 'Pozidriv' wood screw is becoming increasingly popular in woodworking and Fig. 2 page 38 shows 'Pozidriv' screw heads and driver.

There are different metals used in the manufacture of screws, the chief ones being steel, brass and silicon bronze. Screws can also be bright zinc plated or made of nylon.

Brass Cups: Are used for neatness and on work where screws have to be removed occasionally, see E and F.
Fitting Brass Cups and Screws: It is advisable to bore into a scrap piece of wood and test the diameter and depth of hole required for the cups. The cups are driven into the holes and should finish flush with the surface. A depth gauge fitted to the bit controls the depth of boring. A cup which is fitted with its top edge below the surface of the wood constitutes poor workmanship.

To prevent brass screws from shearing, and to keep the slots free from burr, drive in steel screws first. Then

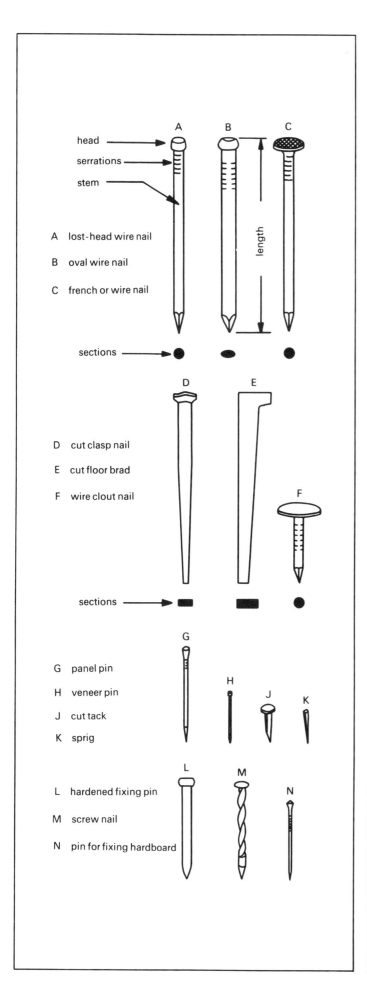

head
serrations
stem

A   lost-head wire nail

B   oval wire nail

C   french or wire nail

length

sections

D   cut clasp nail

E   cut floor brad

F   wire clout nail

sections

G   panel pin

H   veneer pin

J   cut tack

K   sprig

L   hardened fixing pin

M   screw nail

N   pin for fixing hardboard

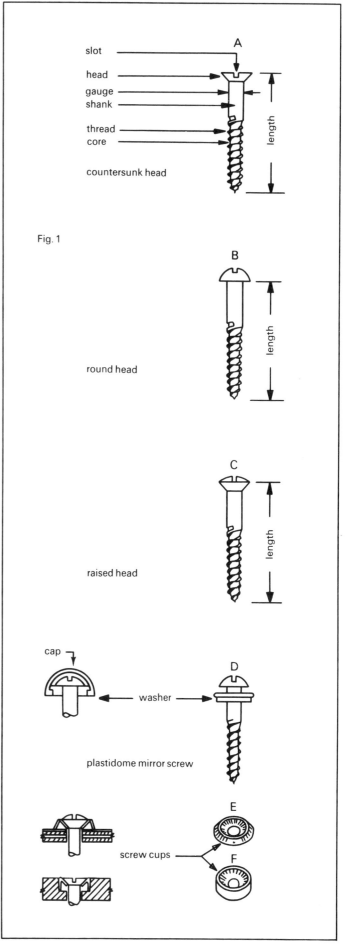

slot
head
gauge
shank
thread
core

length

countersunk head

Fig. 1

round head

length

raised head

length

cap

washer

plastidome mirror screw

screw cups

remove and replace them with brass screws. Dipping the thread of steel or brass screws in petroleum jelly assists in the driving and removing of screws, and prevents steel screws rusting.

Hinging

A wide variety of cabinet fittings is available for the woodworker and new types of hinges, locks and fittings for knock-down furniture are continually being produced to meet the demands of large-scale production of furniture. However, the traditional types of hinges and fittings are still used in the production of first-class and largely hand-made furniture.

Fitting Hinges

Procedure for fitting a door to a carcase. See diagram page 39. (Horns are left on at this stage.)

1 Shoot hanging stile to fit carcase.

2 Plane door to width, working carefully to ensure equal width of stiles and making a slight angle on the inside to prevent binding.

3 Remove horns and plane bottom edge to fit carcase.

4 Plane top edge and fit to carcase. The door should be fitted so as to allow a thin piece of veneer to be slipped under the bottom rail. A piece of cartridge paper makes a good gauge for the width clearance.

Procedure for fitting butts

According to the height and thickness, a door may need two or more butts to give adequate support. When properly fitted, hinges should look right and enhance the job. For panelled and framed doors the top hinge is positioned below the top rail, and the bottom hinge is above the bottom rail, as shown in the diagram on page 39. The hinges on a flush door of the same size would be located in a similar position.

1 Protect door with a piece of baize and place in vice. Mark out position of butts in pencil and cut lines.

2 Set marking gauges to give centre and knuckle thickness respectively and carefully gauge on hanging stile.

3 Make saw kerfs with dovetail saw and chisel out waste.

4 Fit in butts and screw to stile.

5 Place door in aperture, with flanges out. Slip a thin piece of veneer under the bottom rail to give the necessary clearance.

6 Mark the position of the butts on the carcase side. Adjust gauge to allow for 'set in' of door and gauge for flanges. Use a pencil to mark face line of door at butt recesses.

7 Remove waste and fit butts. Fix with one screw in each and try door. Adjust as necessary and complete screwing. Note the alternative hinging positions shown at A, B, C and D page 38, see also diagrams on page 39.

The hinge position as shown at B is commonly used. Here the 'set in' of the door breaks the line and produces a pleasing effect. This 'set in' slightly decreases the amount of opening, as seen in diagram B. The positions given at C and D are suitable for small boxes and chests.

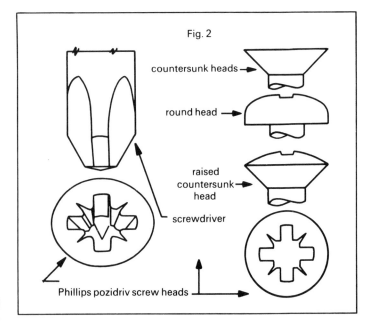

Fig. 2

countersunk heads

round head

raised countersunk head

screwdriver

Phillips pozidriv screw heads

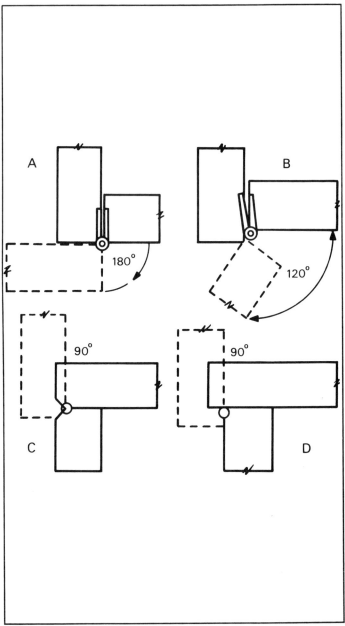

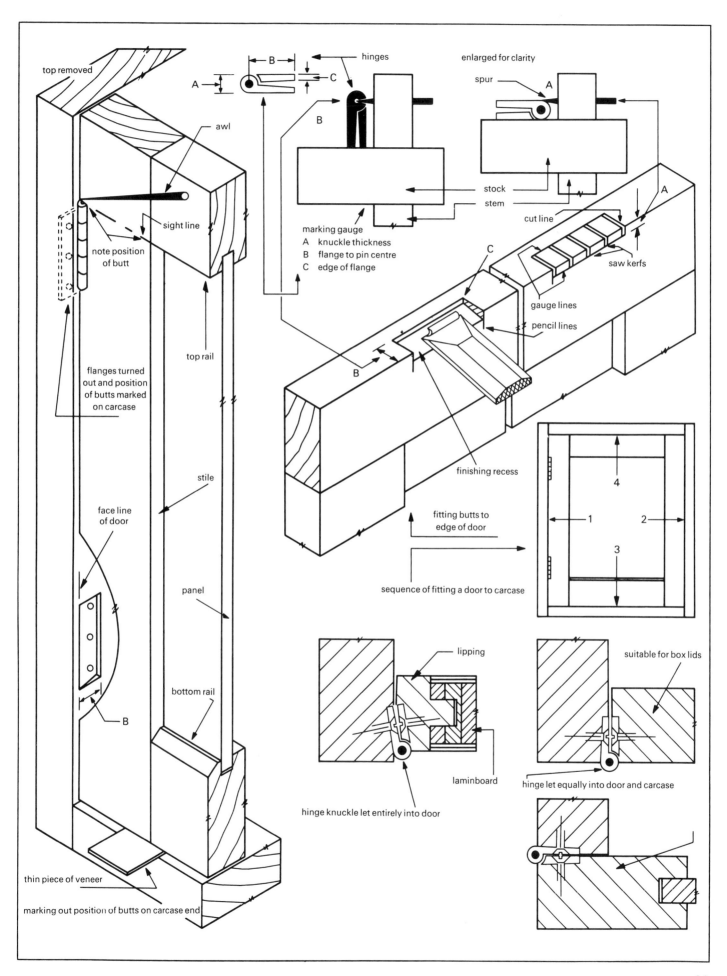

top removed

awl

sight line

note position
of butt

flanges turned
out and position
of butts marked
on carcase

top rail

stile

face line
of door

panel

B

bottom rail

thin piece of veneer

marking out position of butts on carcase end

B

A

C

hinges

B

marking gauge
A knuckle thickness
B flange to pin centre
C edge of flange

enlarged for clarity

spur

A

stock

stem

cut line

A

saw kerfs

gauge lines

pencil lines

C

B

finishing recess

fitting butts to
edge of door

sequence of fitting a door to carcase

1   2

4

3

lipping

laminboard

hinge knuckle let entirely into door

suitable for box lids

hinge let equally into door and carcase

39

Fittings

A selection of hinges and fittings is shown on page 41.

Fig. 1 Brass Butts: solid drawn. A large range of sizes is available for doors, boxes, tables, etc. Butts are obtainable in a variety of metals, the chief ones being brass and steel. Brass butts, solid drawn, are of excellent quality, and are used for first-class work. A much cheaper hinge is the pressed brass type. Nylon hinges are also available.

Fig. 2 Back Flaps: The flanges of these hinges are wider than the normal butt to provide a large bearing surface for extra strength area when screwing. Widely used for table and desk flaps. Fig. 8, 9 and 10 show three methods of fitting back flaps for various rebated falls and flaps.

Fig. 3 Strap Hinge: For narrow sections and where only limited space is available for the hinge.

Fig. 4 Counter Flap Hinge: Counter flaps allow counters to be lifted up and over, and have the advantage of a flush surface, with no projecting knuckles.

Fig. 5 Card Table Hinges: Similar in construction to the counter flaps, but lighter and can be purchased for top face fixing or edge fixing as shown in Fig. 5A.

Fig. 6 Rule Joint Hinge: Used for fall flaps mainly on tables, etc. Fig. 7 gives the setting-out for the hinge. It will be seen from the diagram that the countersinking for the screws is on the reverse side of the knuckle and that the pin centre is placed in the centre of the quadrant describing the moulding. When fitting, the pin should be moved fractionally to the right, see A; this should prevent any tendency to bind when the flap is operated, see also page 45, Fig. 7, for modern type of table hinge.

Wine cabinet in rosewood veneer and solids, 1,065mm (3ft 6in) wide ×455mm (1ft 6in) deep ×1,370mm (4ft 6in) high. Photograph by courtesy of Archie Shine Ltd. See also page 118 giving line diagrams and useful sizes for drinks cabinets, etc.

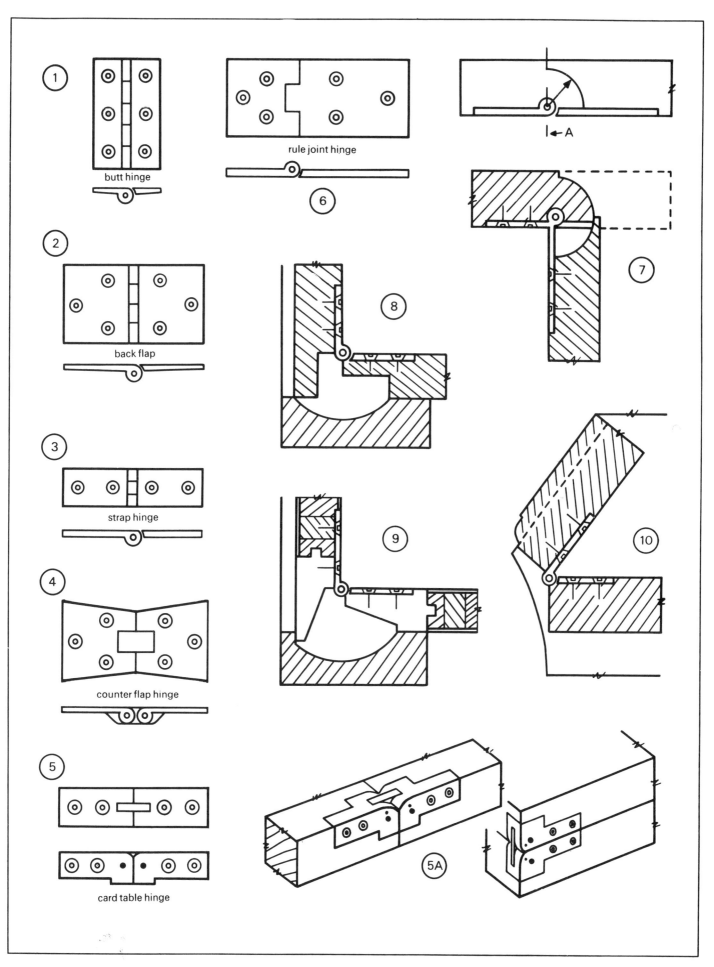

1. butt hinge

2. back flap

3. strap hinge

4. counter flap hinge

5. card table hinge

5A

6. rule joint hinge

7.

8.

9.

10.

A

41

Centre or pivot hinges

Centre Hinges: Fig. 1, page 43, shows one part of an ordinary centre or pivot hinge let into the top edge of a door. Fig. 2 is a view of both parts, and a washer to give clearance when opening or closing is shown placed over the pin. In some makes the washer is an integral part. Before fitting centre hinges it is advisable to make a full-size detail drawing to determine the exact position of the pin, Fig. 3 and 3A.

Two angles of 45° are drawn from the intersecting lines of the door and the inside line of the carcase end; the intersecting point locates the pin centre. If hinged on this point the door should move through an angle of 90° and stop at right angles to the carcase. The hinge can be moved slightly to allow for a small clearance to prevent binding between door and carcase.

Fig. 3A shows a superior method of fitting; in this case the stile is masked by a projecting lip.

In a situation where the top and bottom of the carcase are fixed, the top part of the hinge is held in position while the door is guided into position as shown in Fig. 4 and then fixed.

Fig. 5 and 6 show the opening and closed positions of a door hung with necked or cranked hinges. Fig. 7 shows a door with a necked hinge arranged to open through an angle of 270°.

Tall storage cabinets in teak veneers with double folding doors. The interior is lined with teak and is fitted with five shelves and four removable trays on nylon runners – all adjustable. Cabinet on the left has doors and ends in white melamine.
Designed by: Brian Long, M.S.I.A., and made by Heal Furniture Ltd.
Photograph by courtesy of Heal and Son Ltd.

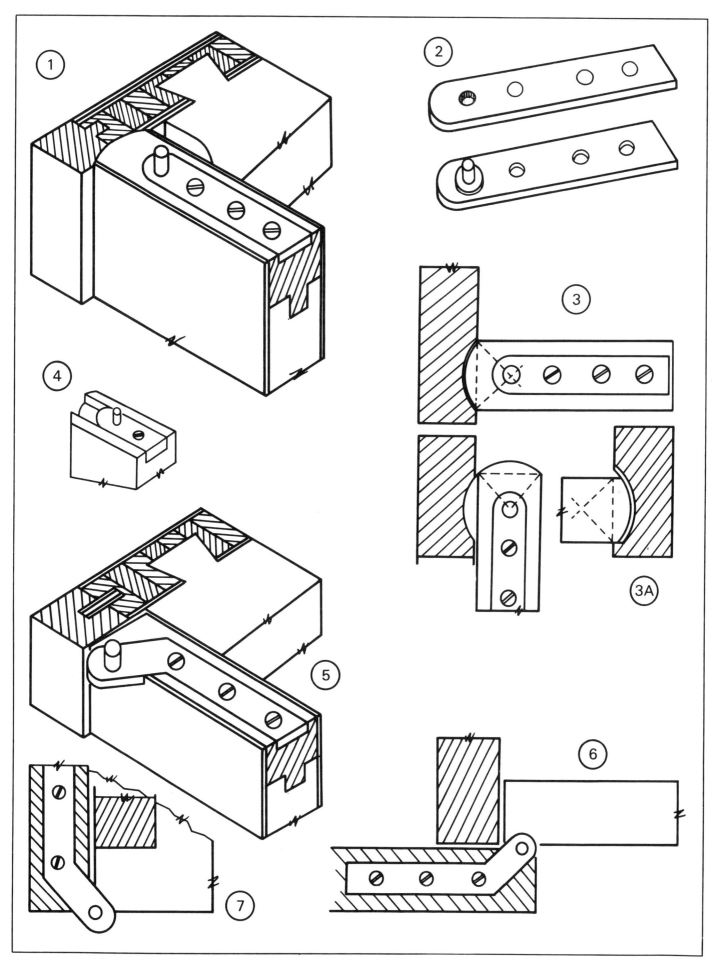

43

Special hinges

The diagrams on page 45 show a selection of special hinges. Fig. 1 shows the location of an angled cabinet hinge, ordinary butts could be used in this situation but the advantage of the angled hinge is obvious. Fig. 1A shows the angled cabinet hinge.

Fig. 2 and 2A give details of the three leaf hinge. The centre leaf which penetrates the division is drilled for pins, and their position depends on the thickness of doors. This type of hinge allows a pair of doors to be hung on a single division. This arrangement produces a neat and pleasing elevation. This type of hinge can be obtained with two or three leaves, and Fig. 3 shows the application of the two leaf pattern.

Fig. 4 and 4A show a superior quality decorative cranked hinge which gives an opening of 270°.

Fig. 5 and 5A give details of a cranked hinge suitable for rebated doors, largely used in kitchen furniture.

Fig. 6 and 6A show the general application of a Soss type of secret hinge (no knuckle seen).

Fig. 7 and 7A give details of the improved table flap hinge. It is advisable to make a trial run before using on the actual job.

Fig. 8 illustrates the Hurlinge. Owing to its special construction the hinge is self-aligning and requires no letting in.

Fig. 9 and 9A show a similar type of hinge which requires no letting in. Types 8 and 9 are widely used in the building and furniture-making industries.

Fall front cabinet. The exterior is of light beech, solid and veneered. Doors and flaps are plastic laminate in antique white. Hinges and handles of solid brass, stove lacquered.
Designed by: Ray Leigh, A.A.Dip., F.S.I.A.; Trevor Chinn; and Martin Hall, M.S.I.A.; and made by Gordon Russell Ltd. Photograph by courtesy of Gordon Russell Ltd.

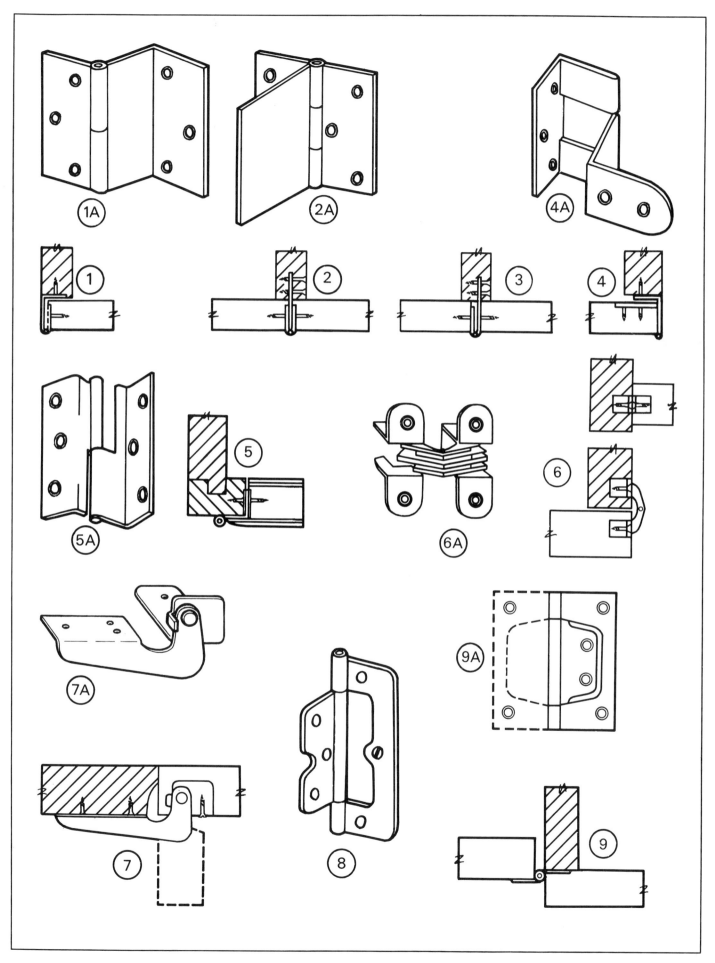

Locks

Locks or catches are required to secure wardrobes, cupboards, sliding doors and drawers, etc. There is a large variety of locks available and care should be taken when designing specific pieces of furniture to see that the fitting is functional and best suited for the purpose for which it is required. The present tendency is to omit locks wherever possible.

The illustrations on pages 47 and 49 give a variety of locks.

Fig. 1 shows the straight cupboard lock. This is screwed to the inner face of the door; it has a bolt which shoots left or right as required.

Fig. 2 shows the cut cupboard lock, this is superior to the straight cupboard lock and is let into the wood. These locks are made right and left-handed. The illustration shows a left-handed lock.

Fig. 3 and 3A show a mortise cupboard lock, left-hand illustrated.

Fig. 4 shows a cut drawer or till lock.

Fig. 5 shows a cut box lock and striking plate.

Fig. 6 and 6A show a mortise cupboard lock for a sliding door; left-hand illustrated. Sliding cut cupboard door locks are also obtainable.

Fig. 7 and 7A show a link plate cupboard lock, double-handed pattern. This type of lock is used when the door closes over the cupboard cheeks or ends.

Fig. 8 and 8A give details of a sliding cut cupboard door lock, with hook bolt at back. Left-hand illustrated.

Fig. 12, shown below, gives details of fitting a drawer lock.

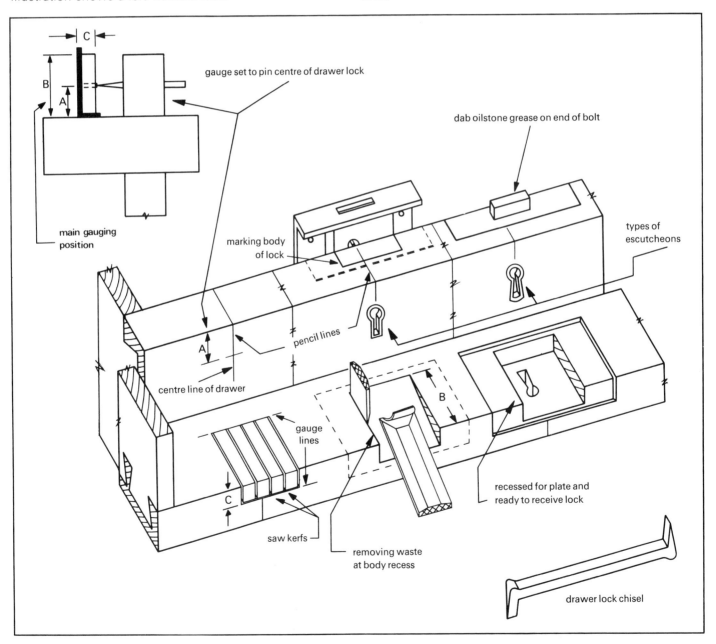

gauge set to pin centre of drawer lock

main gauging position

dab oilstone grease on end of bolt

types of escutcheons

marking body of lock

pencil lines

centre line of drawer

gauge lines

saw kerfs

removing waste at body recess

recessed for plate and ready to receive lock

drawer lock chisel

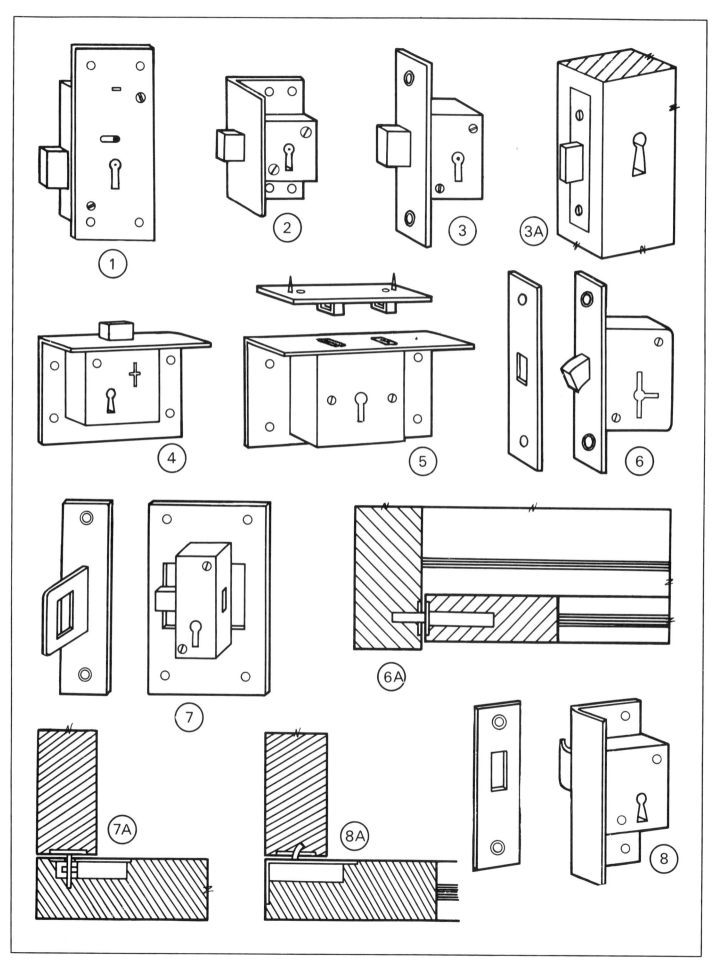

Fig. 9 (page 49) shows the brass piano mortise lock.

Fig. 10 shows a rolltop desk lock.

Fig. 11 shows a simple sliding door lock in polished brass.

Stays

The illustrations on page 49 give details of stays suitable for supporting falls of secretaires, music stools, cabinet lids, etc. These can be obtained right or left-handed.

Fig. 1 and 1A show the rule joint stay, and method of setting-out. To fix stay, take half the length from pin to pin and mark off from 'A' knuckle of back flap hinge —B and C. Then fit plate at C and draw a line from B at right angles to fall as shown. The remaining plate is fixed with its centre exactly on the line squared from B. See back flaps page 41.

Fig. 2 shows a quadrant stay. The diagrams show method of fixing.

Fig. 3 shows a slotted wardrobe or fall stay. An improved type of straight stay is shown in Fig. 5. It runs in a nylon bush.

Fig. 4 shows the fixing of an improved type of fall or flap stay.

Wall furniture, finished in teak, with either teak or white, orange or green painted front panels.
Surfaces are matt and stain resistant. All the backs and drawer bottoms are in off-white melamine.
Designed by: Robert Heritage, R.D.I., Des. R.C.A., F.S.I.A.
Photograph by courtesy of Heal and Son Ltd.

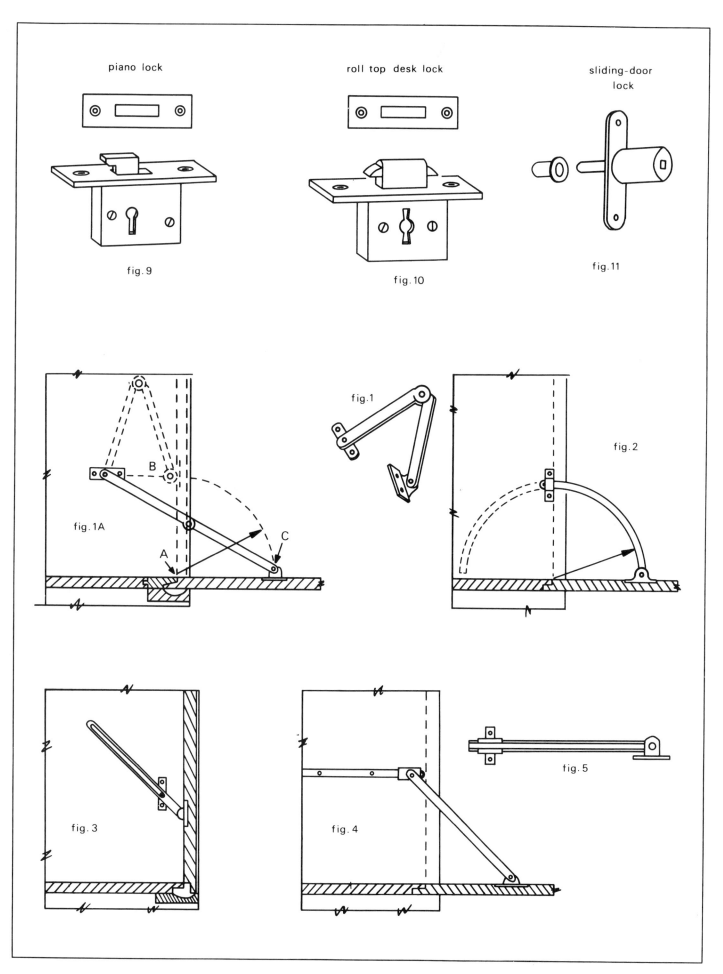

piano lock

roll top desk lock

sliding-door
lock

fig.9

fig.10

fig.11

fig.1

fig.2

fig.1A

A

B

C

fig.3

fig.4

fig.5

49

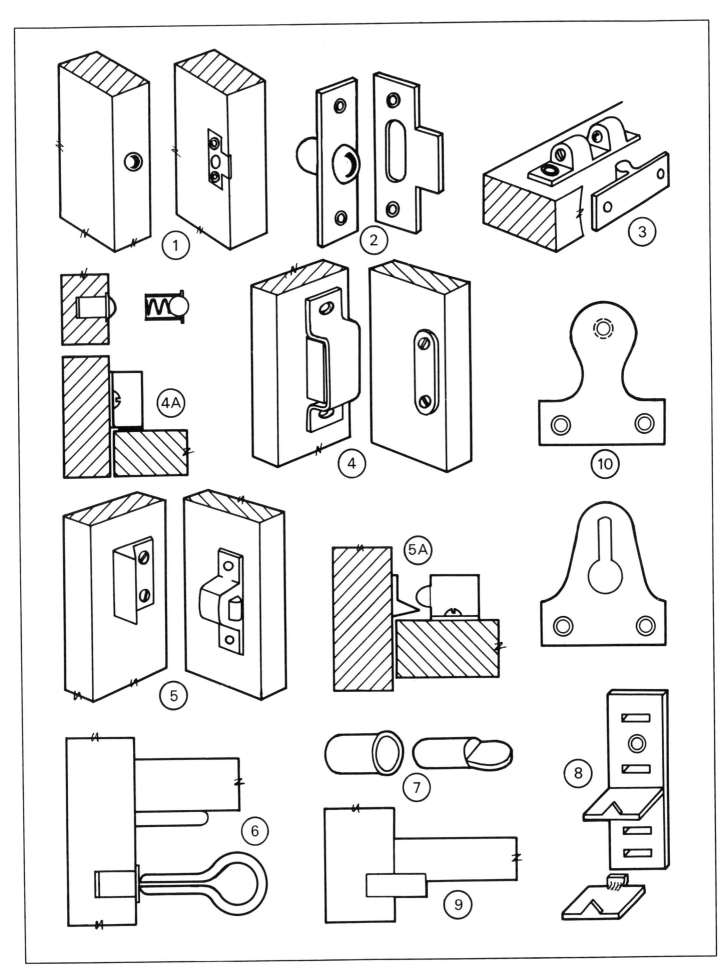

Catches

The illustrations on pages 50 and 51 show a range of catches and useful miscellaneous fittings.

Fig. 1 shows details of a ball catch.

Fig. 2 shows a rather heavier type of catch known as the 'Bales' catch.

Fig. 3 shows the double ball catch; it has the advantage of being easily adjusted for compression.

Fig. 4 and 4A show the popular face fixing magnetic catch and striking plate.

Fig. 5 and 5A show the fixing position of a plastic rocker catch. These catches are durable and quite suitable for small cupboard doors.

Fig. 6, 7, 8 and 9 show methods of fitting adjustable loose shelving for bookcases, cupboards, etc.

Fig. 6 and 7 give details of the stud and socket method.

Fig. 8 is the type known as the 'Tonk strip'.

Fig. 9, dowel pegs, with underside of shelf bored out to fit and locate.

Fig. 10 shows two types of mirror plates, used for fixing bookcases, wall cabinets and mirrors.

Fig. 11. In this case the shelf has stopped grooves in the ends and slides out on hardwood strips which are made to project to suit depth of the groove.

Also shown in Fig. 11 is a stout wire fitting which is pushed into locating holes. The shelf is slid on to the wire.

Fig. 12 shows a flush bolt.

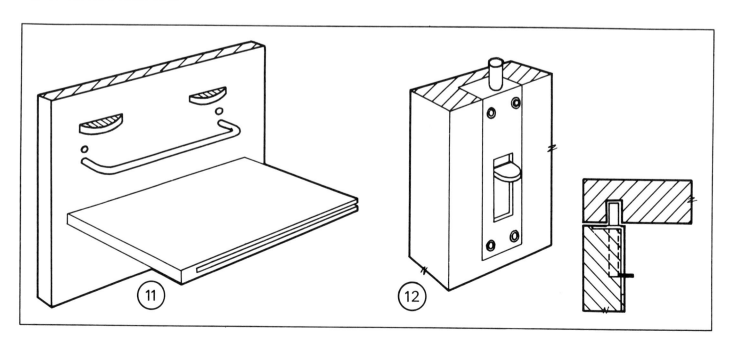

Castors and glides

A wide variety of castors and wheels to suit light cabinet work and heavier industrial needs are available to the designer-craftsman.

Fig. 1 and 1A show a spring peg castor, and section showing method of fixing.

Fig. 2 shows the adjustable Plastiglide.

Fig. 3 shows the Orbit swivel castor.

Sliding doors

There exists a wide range of fittings suitable for sliding doors of various weights and sizes to suit most requirements. Three simple methods quite suitable for cabinet work are shown on page 53. Fig. 1 shows a section through a carcase, with plough grooves to receive plywood doors. Note the extra depth of top grooves to allow for removal. Fig. 2 shows doors mounted on a fibre track whch is let into the carcase, and Fig. 2A shows an enlarged detail of a nylon slide. These slides are let into the bottom of door. Top of door is held by retractable guide pins which run in a fibre track.

Fig. 3 shows one method of fitting sliding glass doors, using fibre tracks which are let into the carcase. It is preferable to have all edges of the glass ground. Glass doors will run smoothly in plough grooves although if in constant use it is advisable to fit a thin fibre or Formica strip into bottom of grooves.

Knock-down fittings

A large proportion of modern furniture is manufactured in ready-to-assemble precision-made units. This method, when distributing or exporting, saves considerable cargo space. Another important factor is its ease of assembly, which can be achieved by unskilled labour. The fittings required to assemble this type of furniture have been developed to suit various conditions found in the industry, and are made in metal and nylon.

Furniture such as chairs, when assembled with the type of fitting illustrated in Fig. 4, would be considered as permanent structures and as such would be classified as 'knock-up fittings'. Furniture which has to be frequently dismantled would be known as 'knock-down', and one suitable fitting for quick and easy dismantling is shown in Fig. 6.

Fig. 4–7 show a range of metal fittings and these are generally grouped in three categories.
1 Threaded fittings as shown in Fig. 4; these can be used for beds and chairs.
2 Interlocking type, by which components are screwed or knocked together. These can be obtained with flat or angled plates and screws as shown in Fig. 5.
3 Cam action fittings as illustrated in Fig. 6 and 6A. Fig. 7 and 7A show details of a useful type of fitting which has a bush fixing plate and screw, and face fitting screw cups.

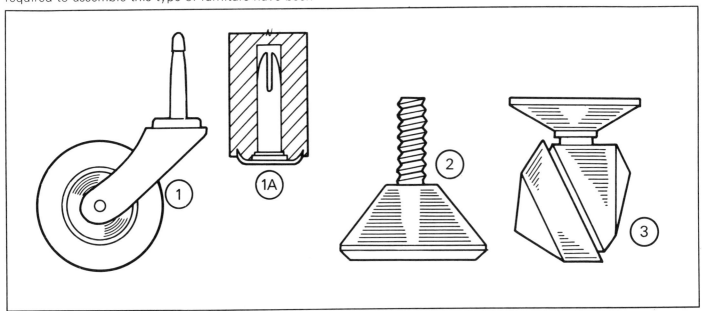

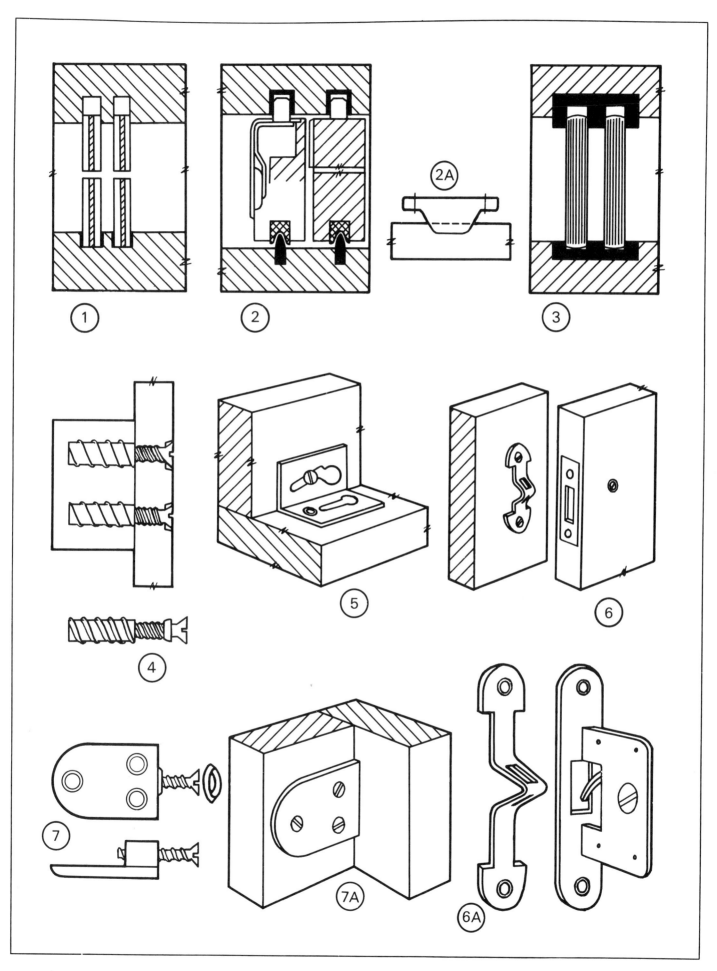

Construction and design development

The work in this and the following section, 'Designs', has been planned and arranged to assist the potential designer or craftsman to solve specific problems. A wide variety of information dealing with specifications, cutting lists, joint planning and setting-out for hand or machine work is included.

There are numerous photographs and exploded views showing methods of construction, and detailed drawings of suitable joints for a range of woodwork projects. These are shown in a variety of projections — orthographic, oblique, isometric, axonometric, and perspective.[1]

A selection of model furniture is included.

Every opportunity should be taken to study the historical background and development of the use of wood in building and for furniture and the way changing fashions, social conditions, and the introduction of new materials, processes and techniques available today offer tremendous scope to versatile designer-craftsmen.

The designer cannot have too much information on timber — its strength, workability, colour, weight, availability — or its various 'man-made' forms such as veneers, plywood, laminated and blockboards, chipboard, plastic-faced sheets, in which it is now obtainable.

Knowledge of metal fittings — methods of upholstery and the material used — in fact, as wide an acquaintance as possible with processes and materials of all kinds is also an essential part of the designer's equipment. In addition to this knowledge, the designer must also possess originality, inspiration and good judgement, for without these qualitites he cannot make the best use of his knowledge.

[1] For information on drawing presentation see page 102.

The work has been arranged to cover, as well as possible, construction and design development in general; and it is with hopeful optimism that it will be used simply as a foundation to good design.

General design considerations

It is obviously an advantage for the designer to have some of the qualities outlined in the above introduction. He may also have a natural gift or flair for design or perhaps he has worked to develop his talents in this direction. It is desirable to have an understanding of the principles of ergonomics — the study of human mental and physical performance in work situations, in terms of efficiency and competence — and of anthropometrics — the science concerned with the measurement of man.

Everything we create is based on our knowledge and experience; a study of architecture helps us to appreciate good proportion. Experience in one or more of the woodworking crafts gives the designer an opportunity to learn something of the intricacies of construction, and the various component arrangements it is possible to create with carcases, stools, legs, doors, drawers, handles, and many other features. He should also be familiar with the technique of hand and machine production, so that he would be aware of industrial practice and requirements.

General observations on design
Much has already been written on design methods, but I hope that these general observations and the foregoing comments will be of some assistance to all those interested in designing articles in wood or metal.
1 The precise details of the assignment or problem must be clearly stated; this should include the purpose and essential requirements of the article or articles.
2 Preparation of design brief. From the information given, prepare a written analysis of the problem to include facts, figures, sources of information, including books, magazines, etc.
3 Research. Make use of reference books. Experiment with shapes, visual forms, texture, patterns, etc. Examine and measure similar articles. Select the most suitable materials for the job, considering colour harmony in relation to mass.
4 Collect and collate all relevant material and

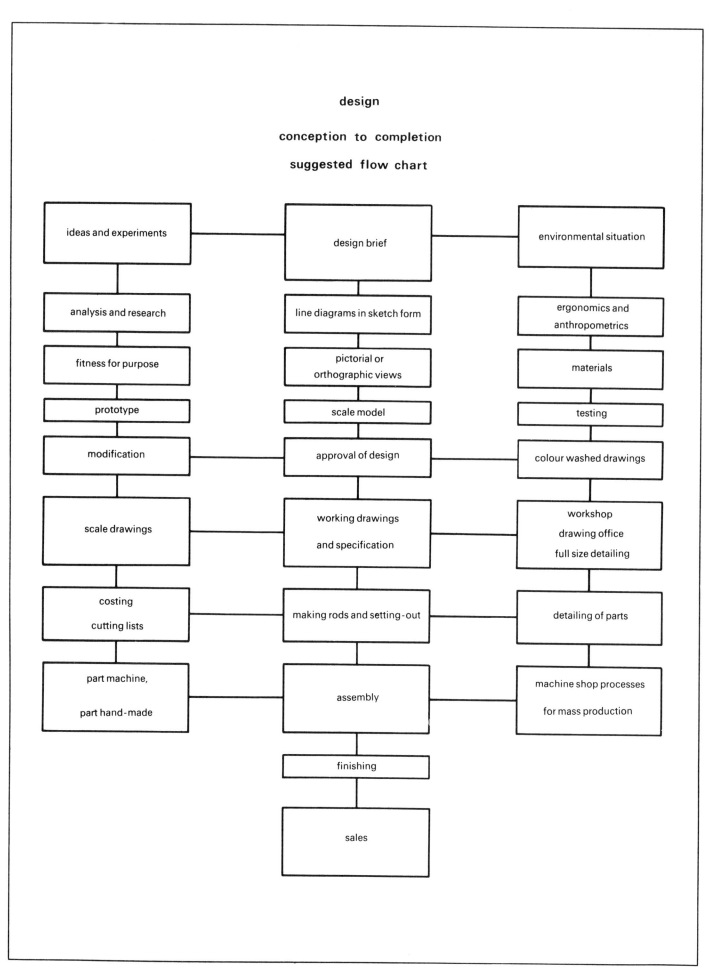

design

conception to completion

suggested flow chart

ideas and experiments	design brief	environmental situation
analysis and research	line diagrams in sketch form	ergonomics and anthropometrics
fitness for purpose	pictorial or orthographic views	materials
prototype	scale model	testing
modification	approval of design	colour washed drawings
scale drawings	working drawings and specification	workshop drawing office full size detailing
costing cutting lists	making rods and setting-out	detailing of parts
part machine, part hand-made	assembly	machine shop processes for mass production
	finishing	
	sales	

information, and make selection from this. Include standard sizes, which long usage has proved satisfactory.

5 It is interesting to note that many functional shapes are naturally streamlined, for example a propellor blade, a ship's hull, a dart, parts of cars, the aeroplane, etc. Generally, all well-finished articles should be smooth and of a clean line. They must be well made, look and feel right, so as to function satisfactorily.

6 Ultimate aim — to create an original interpretation of a given assignment.

Suggested design stages

1 The design brief must be fully understood before proceeding with the planning of a solution.

2 Make numerous line diagrams — in sketch form (see notes dealing with sketching below).

3 Check brief for specification, measurements, written analysis and other relevant material.

4 Resolve details still in tentative form, make sketches in pictorial and orthographic views.

5 Make model to scale, check proportions and any unusual working parts. Modify if necessary. Draw full-size details as necessary. Drawing and model-making assist the designer in explaining to other people the character of his ideas.

6 Production of prototype (not always necessary as model could give sufficient information).

7 Production of full working drawings to scale. Include full-size details as necessary. See notes below.

8 Perspective drawings — colour washed.

9 Estimated cost of job. See Flow Chart page 55.

Notes on working drawings

After completing his preliminary investigation, research and development of his assignments, the designer produces drawings and specifications for workshop use.

A working drawing is usually a scale drawing of a design, giving all the necessary information and data for the craftsman's use. This should include essential features and full-size details. Orthographic, oblique, isometric, axonometric and perspective views are all methods which can be usefully employed for illustration by the designer.

Notes on sketching

Sketching is a means by which an idea may be illustrated and developed rapidly, and to be able to sketch competently is a great asset to the designer-craftsman. It needs constant practice to become really efficient and it is worthwhile developing the habit of carrying a sketch book, so that ideas may be readily jotted down.

A good sketch should be annotated and show clearly:

1 Name of piece.

2 General outline and shape of parts.

3 All major dimensions.

4 Special instructions and features.

5 Materials and proposed finishes.

6 Notes on specification.

7 It should be reasonably accurate, regarding scale and proportion.

8 Pictorial sketching has obvious advantages and colour washing enhances appearance.

Frame construction

A *frame* is designed to break up large surface areas of wood into smaller units and thus minimise the effect of shrinkage and warping, and yet provide strength in both length and width. The panelled door shown on page 57 is a good example of frame construction. The drawings show how the main joints — with proportions — are arranged to give maximum strength. The door has raised and fielded panels, and stuck mouldings — that is moulding worked on the material by hand or machine. Note the method of scribing mouldings and the fitting of joints.

A wide variety of doors and panelling are included in this category.

Designing of joints

As the making of joints usually involves the removal of waste, it necessarily follows that the joints must be as strong as possible without unduly weakening any part of the structure.

It is obviously an advantage to have some practical knowledge of construction, strength of materials and the properties of various glues.

Joints: Shown in the drawings on page 57 are: haunched mortise and tenoned joints; two or more single tenons on wide rails, see Fig. 1 page 57; stub or stump tenon.

Special features and suggestions: Stuck ovolo mouldings. Scribed mouldings — scribed mouldings at joint intersections counteract the effect of shrinkage, see Fig. 2 and 3 page 57. Raised and fielded panels as a decorative feature.

Large doors such as that on page 57 are usually made with through mortise and tenon and wedged joints.

When mortise locks are fitted, the lock rail should have twin tenons. For lighter doors such as used in cabinet making, the tenons are usually stopped.

Portion of a gunstock door stile with bedded bolection moulding and fielded panel.

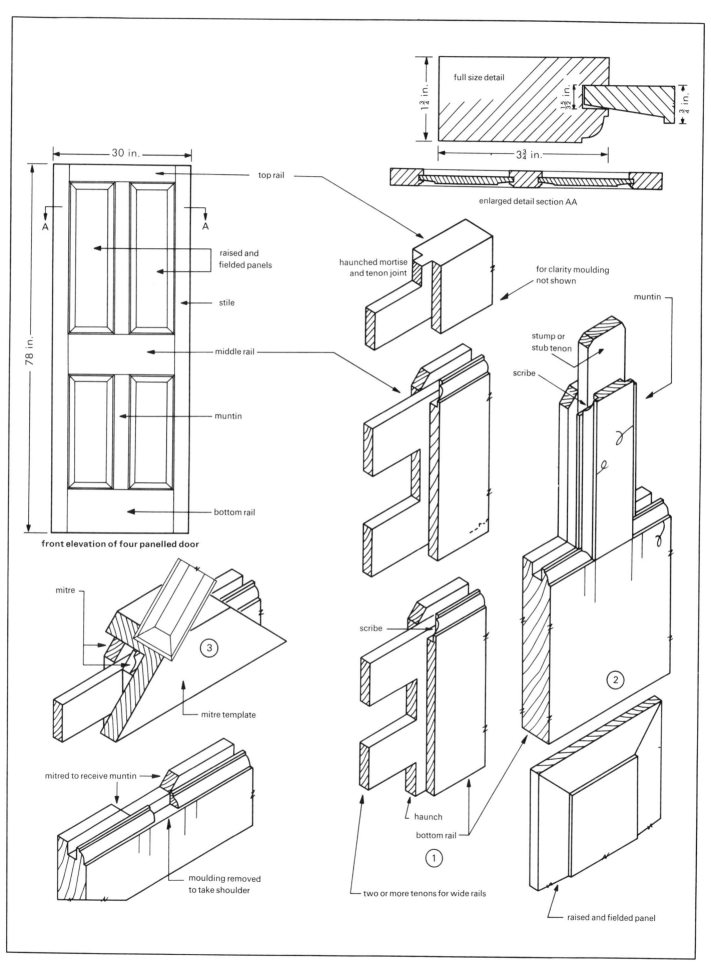

full size detail

$1\frac{3}{4}$ in.

$\frac{15}{32}$ in.

$\frac{3}{4}$ in.

$3\frac{3}{4}$ in.

enlarged detail section AA

30 in.

A   A

78 in.

top rail

raised and
fielded panels

stile

middle rail

muntin

bottom rail

front elevation of four panelled door

haunched mortise
and tenon joint

for clarity moulding
not shown

muntin

stump or
stub tenon

scribe

scribe

mitre

mitre template

mitred to receive muntin

moulding removed
to take shoulder

haunch

bottom rail

two or more tenons for wide rails

raised and fielded panel

①

②

③

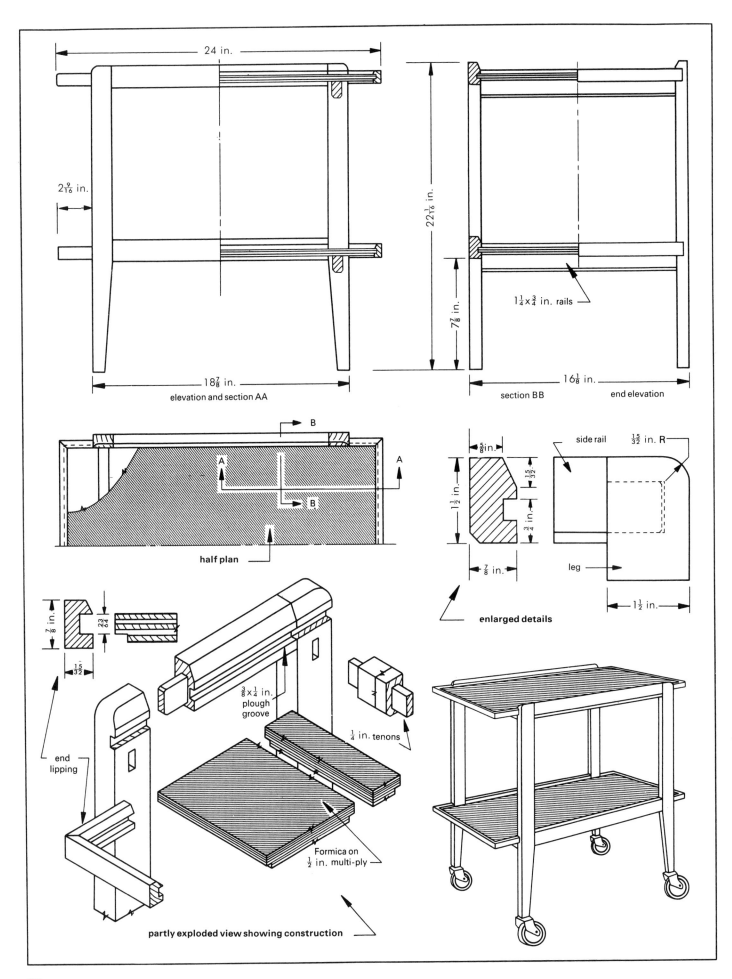

24 in.

$2\frac{9}{16}$ in.

$22\frac{1}{16}$ in.

$7\frac{7}{8}$ in.

$1\frac{1}{4} \times \frac{3}{4}$ in. rails

$18\frac{7}{8}$ in.

elevation and section AA

$16\frac{1}{8}$ in.

section BB   end elevation

B

A   A

B

half plan

$\frac{5}{8}$ in.

$\frac{15}{32}$

$1\frac{1}{2}$ in.

$\frac{3}{4}$

$\frac{7}{8}$ in.

side rail $\frac{15}{32}$ in. R

leg

$1\frac{1}{2}$ in.

enlarged details

$\frac{7}{8}$ in.

$\frac{23}{64}$

$\frac{15}{32}$

end lipping

$\frac{3}{8} \times \frac{1}{4}$ in. plough groove

$\frac{1}{4}$ in. tenons

Formica on $\frac{1}{2}$ in. multi-ply

partly exploded view showing construction

Dinner Waggon

The waggon illustrated on page 58 is an example of frame construction, consisting of two side frames of rectangular sectioned material, connected with end rails and multi-ply shelves.

Joints: Stopped mortise and tenon. Rails ploughed to receive trays.

Special features and suggestions: Formica-faced trays arranged for easy cleaning. Note edge treatment at end of trays, and use of bevels and chamfers as decorative treatment. Consider, lift out trays, and possible use of flaps. A folding waggon. Colour harmony in relation to timber used, and environmental situation. Various types of wheels.

Framed carcase construction

This consists basically of mortised and tenoned frames with panels. The frames can be assembled in a variety of ways to form interesting carcase assemblies. A few variations are shown in the drawings page 60.

Fig. 1 shows a typical framed carcase suitable for sideboard or storage cabinet construction, and alternative end treatments. Designs for various framed ends suitable for desks, writing tables, etc., are shown in Fig. 2.

Constructional details

These are clearly shown in the drawing, Fig. 3. See also pages 26–29 and photographs on pages 59 and 61.

Joints: Mortise and tenon — note application of twin tenons; dowelled; tongue and grooved; lap dovetail; finger joint.

Special features and suggestions: Use of laminboard or chipboard, dowelled or tongued to shaped legs. Various shaped end frames. Consider designing articles shaped in plan, using metal spaces for drawer units, and ideas for opening drawers.

Linen chest in oak with moulded and butted panels.

Portion of framing in teak showing chamfer and intersection of mason's mitre.

Portion of framing in teak with moulded intersection finished with mason's mitre. The panel is fielded.

Exploded view showing a haunched mortise and tenon joint.

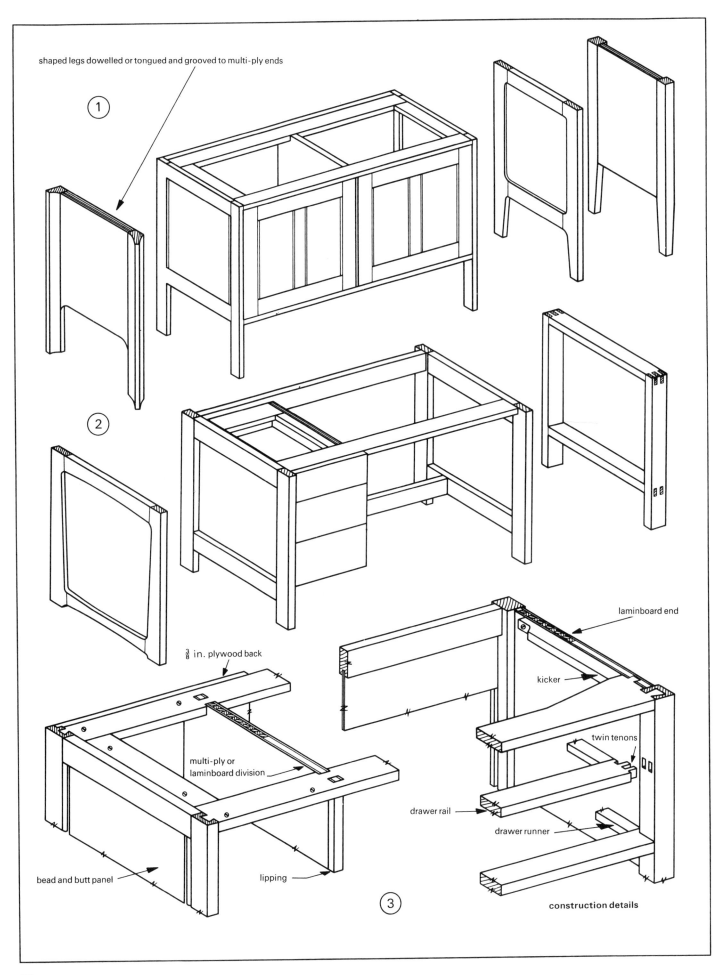

shaped legs dowelled or tongued and grooved to multi-ply ends

(1)

(2)

$\frac{3}{8}$ in. plywood back

multi-ply or
laminboard division

bead and butt panel

lipping

(3)

laminboard end

kicker

twin tenons

drawer rail

drawer runner

construction details

60

Table or framed work

Included under this heading are stools, chairs (see models page 91), tables and stands, which are mainly based on mortise and tenon or dowelled joints.

Stool construction

The drawings on page 62 show constructional details of a dressing stool with a drop-in seat. The stool has square tapered legs and moulded rails, rebated to take the seat.

Note alternative rail sections and plan showing strengthening brackets — a technique frequently used in chair construction (see photograph right).

Joints: Haunched mortise and tenon with mitred intersections. See detail showing leg, rail and tenon proportions. Note: to allow for possible shrinkage, the tenons must not touch at intersection.

Special features and suggestions: The seat has rounded

Dressing stool in utile.

Portion of framing with elliptical head and splayed shoulders. A cavetto moulding is shown worked round framing.

Dressing stool with loose seat removed, showing corner brackets.

Exploded view showing construction.

Secret haunched mortise and tenon joint.

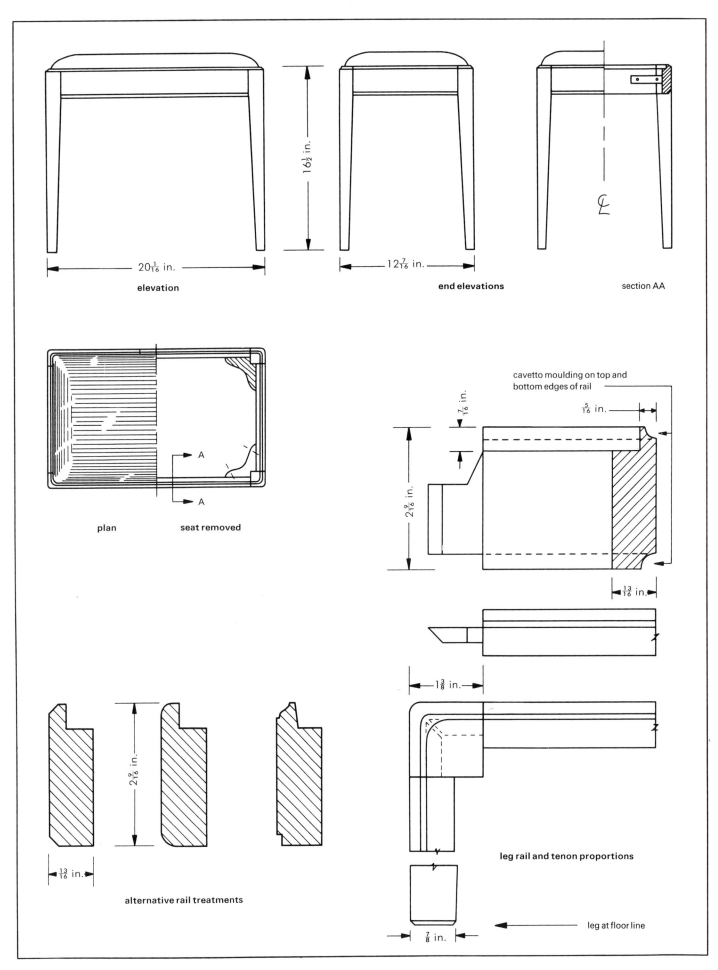

16½ in.

20 1/16 in.

elevation

12 7/16 in.

end elevations

section AA

plan

seat removed

A

A

cavetto moulding on top and
bottom edges of rail

7/16 in.

5/16 in.

2 9/16 in.

1 3/16 in.

1 3/8 in.

leg rail and tenon proportions

2 9/16 in.

1 3/16 in.

alternative rail treatments

7/8 in.

leg at floor line

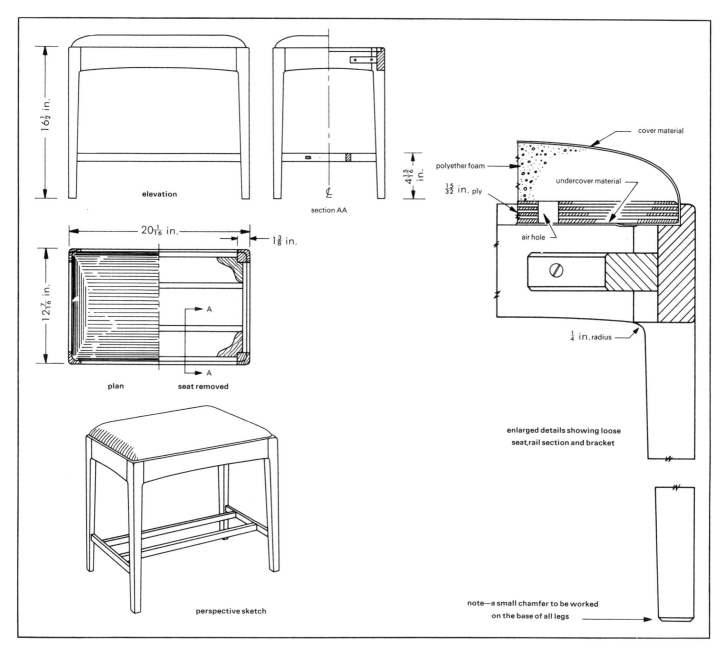

16½ in.

section AA

4 15/16 in.

elevation

20 1/16 in.

1 3/8 in.

12 7/16 in.

plan

seat removed

A

A

cover material

polyether foam

15/32 in. ply

undercover material

air hole

¼ in. radius

enlarged details showing loose
seat, rail section and bracket

note—a small chamfer to be worked
on the base of all legs

perspective sketch

corners to suit radius at top of legs. Rounded corners make a neat and attractive finish to the upholstery.

Consider using rectangular section material — see joint shown on page 61 — for the legs as shown for waggon and small table pages 58 and 65.

Full working drawings and details of a stool with square tapered and shaped legs and rails are given on this page. The stool has an underframing consisting of four rails.

Joints: As in the previous stool. The underframing may have stopped tenons or alternatively through mortise and tenon joints, to make a decorative feature.

Consider various shapes for legs and a shaped laminated underframing.

Cutting list for stool shown on page 62

	Length	Width	Thickness	Material
4 Legs	16¾ in.	1 5/16 in.	1 5/16 in.	Utile
2 Side rails	20 in.	2 9/16 in.	⅞ in.	Utile
2 End rails	12⅜ in.	2 9/16 in.	⅞ in.	Utile
1 piece of plywood for base	19 11/16 in.	12 in.	½ in.	
1 piece of hardwood to make 4 brackets	11 13/16 in.	2 3/16 in.	⅞ in.	Utile Teak or Beech

Seat material: 1 piece of Polyether foam (20 x 12⅜ x 2 in.)

Linen moquette, velvet or other furnishing fabric for seat cover

Linette for underside

Small table with shaped legs (see page 65).

Joints: Stopped mortise and tenon; decorative through mortise and tenon and wedged joint.

Special features and suggestions: Shaped top and lower rails. Tapered legs, decorated with 3mm ×3mm ($\frac{1}{8}$in ×$\frac{1}{8}$in) chamfers.

Note arrangement of joints to allow for maximum strength, and method of working shaped shoulders.

See photograph showing joints for shaped work, right and on page 61.

Refectory tables
Although designed centuries ago, this type of table still remains popular, particularly where space is restricted. With availability of laminboard, veneers, and various finishes this type of table offers considerable design possibilities. Suitable timbers for the table when made in the solid are oak, chestnut and elm.

Joints: Through and stopped mortise and tenon; twin tenons; lap dovetail for top rails.

Special features and suggestions: Basically the table consists of five main components:
1 Two end frames or trusses.
2 Top and bottom connecting rails.
3 A top.

Fig. 1, page 66, gives full details of joint arrangements for end framing, and Fig. 2 shows an alternative design.

The ends could also be made to include panels. The top can be made up of solid wood, framed with flush panels or constructed in laminboard, veneered and lipped. An allowance must be made for shrinkage when fixing solid tops.

The foot and top bearer rails are shaped and the main decorative treatment is the chamfer, it is worth considering the use of sculptured sections, see photograph of model and sculptured joint shown right.

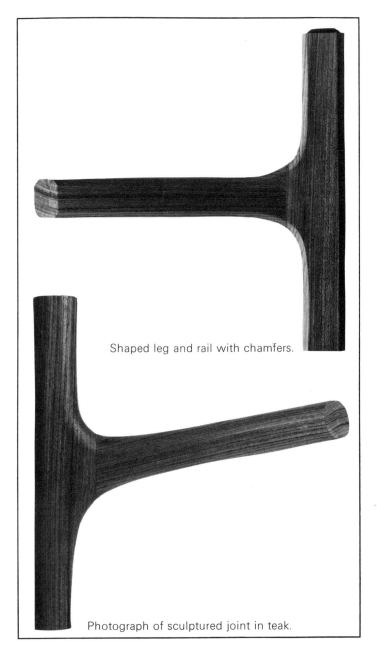

Shaped leg and rail with chamfers.

Photograph of sculptured joint in teak.

Right: Model of refectory table.

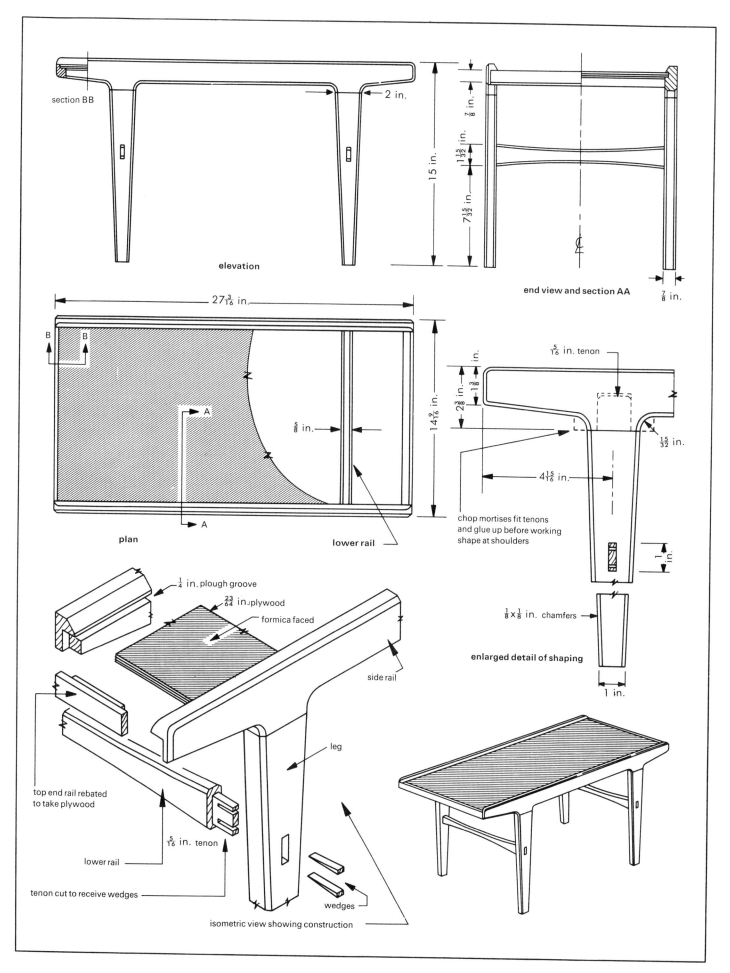

section BB

2 in.

15 in.

elevation

$\frac{7}{8}$ in.

$1\frac{15}{32}$ in.

$7\frac{15}{32}$ in.

end view and section AA

$\frac{7}{8}$ in.

$27\frac{3}{16}$ in.

B   B

A

A

$\frac{5}{8}$ in.

$14\frac{9}{16}$ in.

plan

lower rail

$\frac{5}{16}$ in. tenon

in.

$1\frac{3}{8}$

$2\frac{3}{8}$ in.

$\frac{15}{32}$ in.

$4\frac{15}{16}$ in.

$\frac{1}{2}$ in.

chop mortises fit tenons
and glue up before working
shape at shoulders

$\frac{1}{8} \times \frac{1}{8}$ in. chamfers

enlarged detail of shaping

1 in.

$\frac{1}{4}$ in. plough groove

$\frac{23}{64}$ in. plywood

formica faced

side rail

leg

top end rail rebated
to take plywood

$\frac{5}{16}$ in. tenon

lower rail

tenon cut to receive wedges

wedges

isometric view showing construction

65

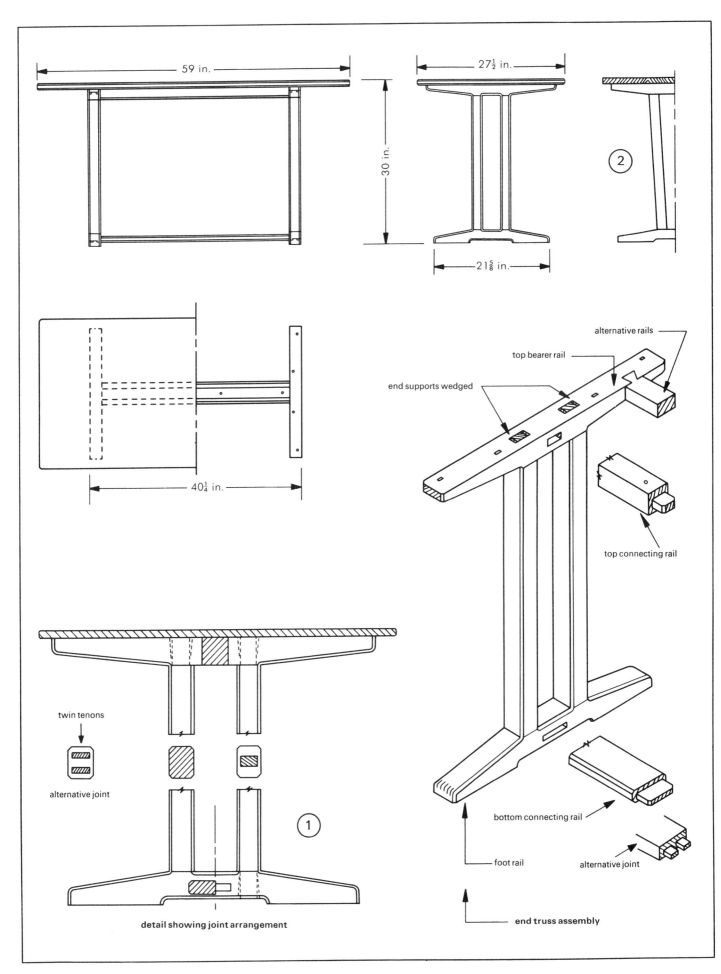

59 in.

27$\frac{1}{2}$ in.

30 in.

21$\frac{5}{8}$ in.

②

40$\frac{1}{4}$ in.

alternative rails

top bearer rail

end supports wedged

top connecting rail

twin tenons

alternative joint

①

bottom connecting rail

foot rail

alternative joint

end truss assembly

detail showing joint arrangement

Small table with drawer

The working drawings on pages 68–69 give full information for the making of a small table with drawer. The drawings show elevation, plan, sectional views and enlarged details of drawer and handles.

Special features and suggestions: Drawer front treatments play an important part in the designing of furniture. The information given in 'drawer details' shows the drawer front 'set in' from the rails. This breaks the line, and produces a feeling of lightness to the drawer rails. It also conceals possible shrinkage, and makes a pleasant shadow line around the drawer front.

A flush treatment can also be obtained, by simply setting back the drawer rails, and making the drawer fronts wider to mask the rails. See pages 86, 89, and 90.

Drawer fronts can be shaped, decorated with inlay, moulded, and veneered, etc.

The small turned handles on the drawer fronts are neat and attractive; also consider flush, metal, and handles that are incorporated in the drawer fronts.

Small table

Constructional details: The exploded views, page 69, give full constructional details of the table illustrated on page 68. The joints are arranged to give maximum strength in relation to the specified material.

Joints: Double mortise and tenon on end rails; twin mortise and tenons at drawer rails (prevents twisting or warping of rail); dovetailing at top front rail and brackets (brackets are particularly useful for stiffening carcases).

Note method of fixing tops. Buttons or metal plates are normally used for fixing solid tops, pocket screwing can be usefully employed in the fixing of laminboard and chipboard tops. See detail Fig. 2.

Drawer stops may be of solid wood or plywood glued and pinned as shown, or of solid wood stops 'mortised in' as shown on page 72.

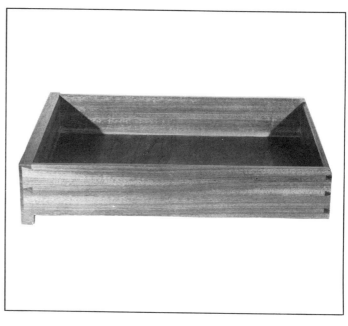

Alternative drawer shown with front made wider to mask drawer rail.

Photograph showing three models in balsa wood and veneer.

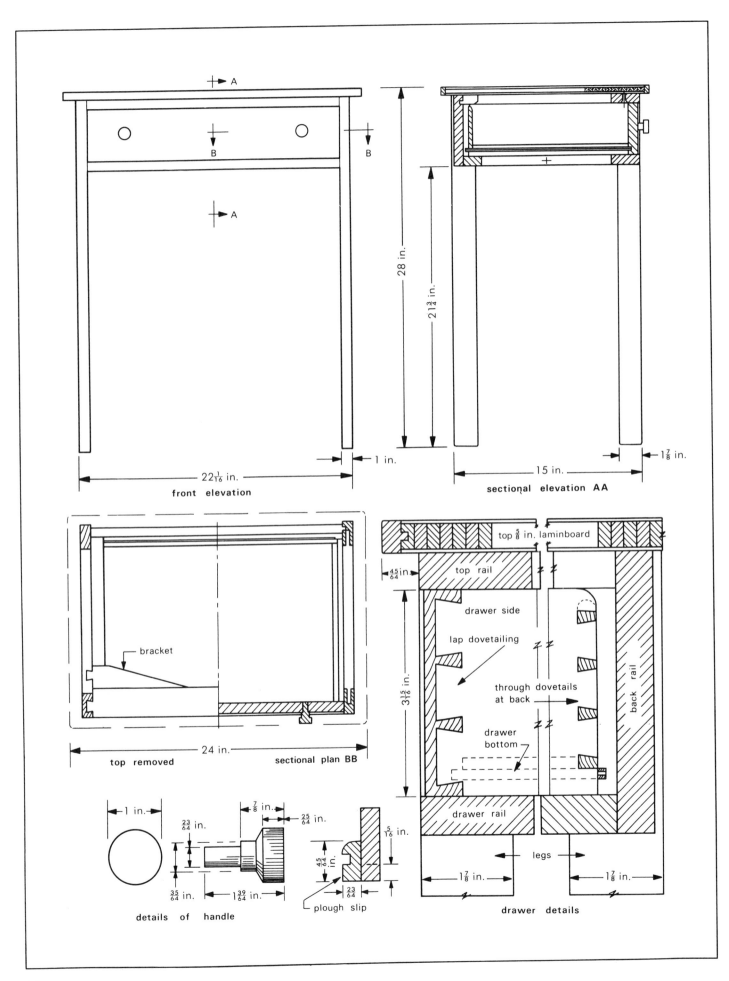

+—— A

B

B

+—— A

28 in.

$21\frac{3}{4}$ in.

1 in.

$22\frac{1}{16}$ in.

front elevation

15 in.

$1\frac{7}{8}$ in.

sectional elevation AA

bracket

24 in.

top removed

sectional plan BB

top $\frac{5}{8}$ in. laminboard

$\frac{45}{64}$ in.

top rail

drawer side

lap dovetailing

through dovetails
at back

back rail

drawer
bottom

$3\frac{15}{16}$ in.

drawer rail

legs

$1\frac{7}{8}$ in.

$1\frac{7}{8}$ in.

drawer details

1 in.

$\frac{23}{64}$ in.

$\frac{7}{8}$ in.

$\frac{25}{64}$ in.

$\frac{5}{16}$ in.

$\frac{45}{64}$ in.

$\frac{35}{64}$ in.

$1\frac{39}{64}$ in.

$\frac{23}{64}$ in.

plough slip

details of handle

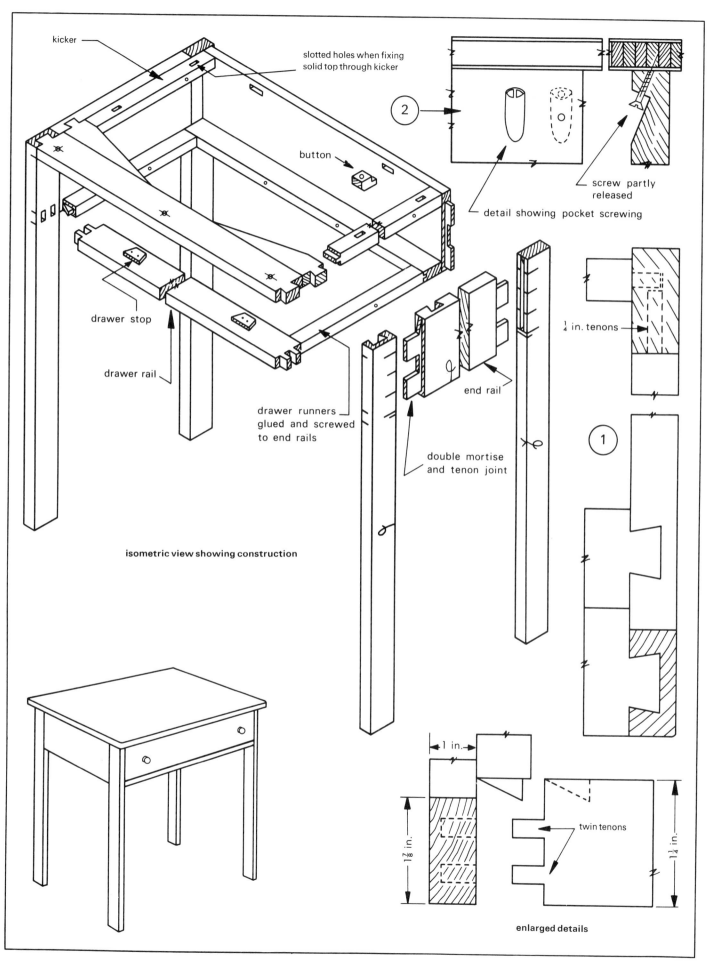

kicker

slotted holes when fixing
solid top through kicker

button

screw partly
released

detail showing pocket screwing

2

drawer stop

drawer rail

drawer runners
glued and screwed
to end rails

end rail

double mortise
and tenon joint

$\frac{1}{4}$ in. tenons

1

isometric view showing construction

1 in.

$1\frac{7}{8}$ in.

$1\frac{1}{4}$ in.

twin tenons

enlarged details

Writing tables

The elevations of four writing tables are shown on page 71. Enlarged details of a handle and integral drawer pull are included. The drawings also show an interesting variety of leg and drawer arrangements.

Special features and suggestions: Shaped, turned, sculptured or moulded legs; shaped, flush and canted drawer fronts; rectangular shaped handle with inlay; inset of leather for top surface.

Design for writing table

Full working drawings of one of the writing tables illustrated on page 71 is given below. Note method of lipping laminboard and top treatment to receive a leather panel.

Setting-out and constructional details of writing table, page 72.

Joints: The isometric drawings give details of mortise and tenon joints for wide rails, and stub tenon for underframing. Note dovetailing at leg and end rails, and arrangement of twin tenons at drawer rails, and vertical division.

The back and end rails are rebated to take the drawer framing.

Special features and suggestions: The drawer sides are slip dovetailed to drawer front to allow for masking of vertical drawer division.

Note method of fixing top, and improved method of making drawer stops; these are shouldered and mortised and glued into the drawer rail.

The dustboards may be of plywood.

The setting-out details should be carefully studied.

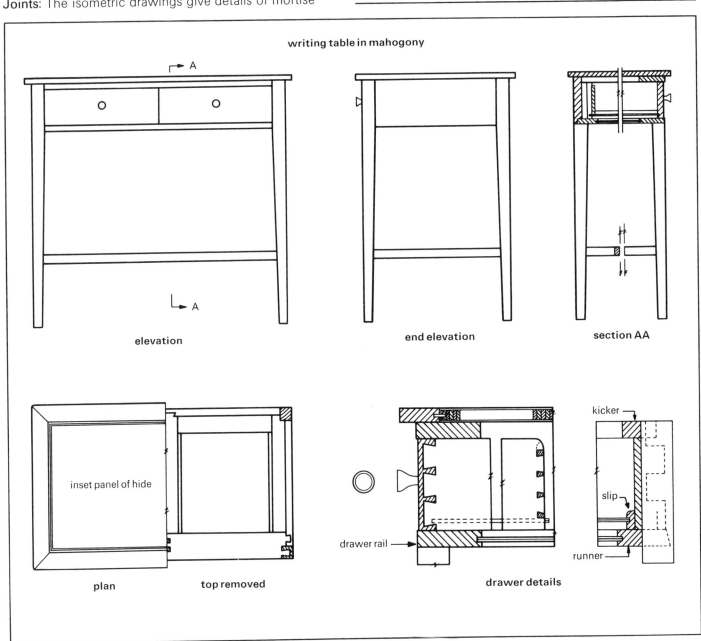

writing table in mahogony

elevation   end elevation   section AA

inset panel of hide

plan   top removed

kicker

drawer rail

slip

runner

drawer details

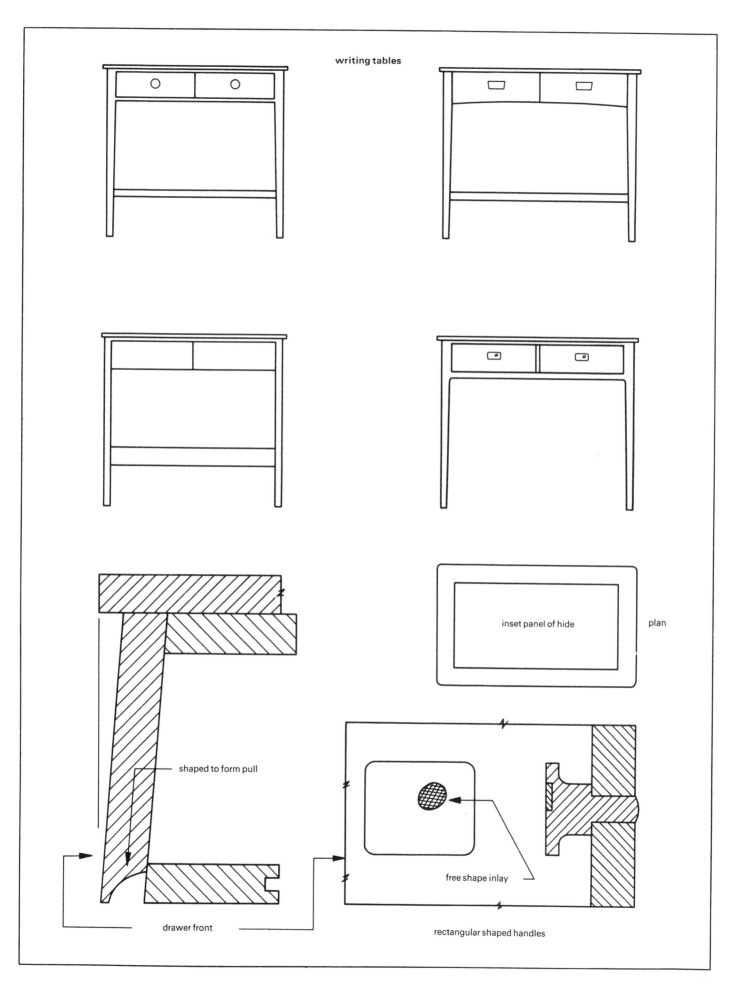

writing tables

shaped to form pull

drawer front

inset panel of hide

plan

free shape inlay

rectangular shaped handles

71

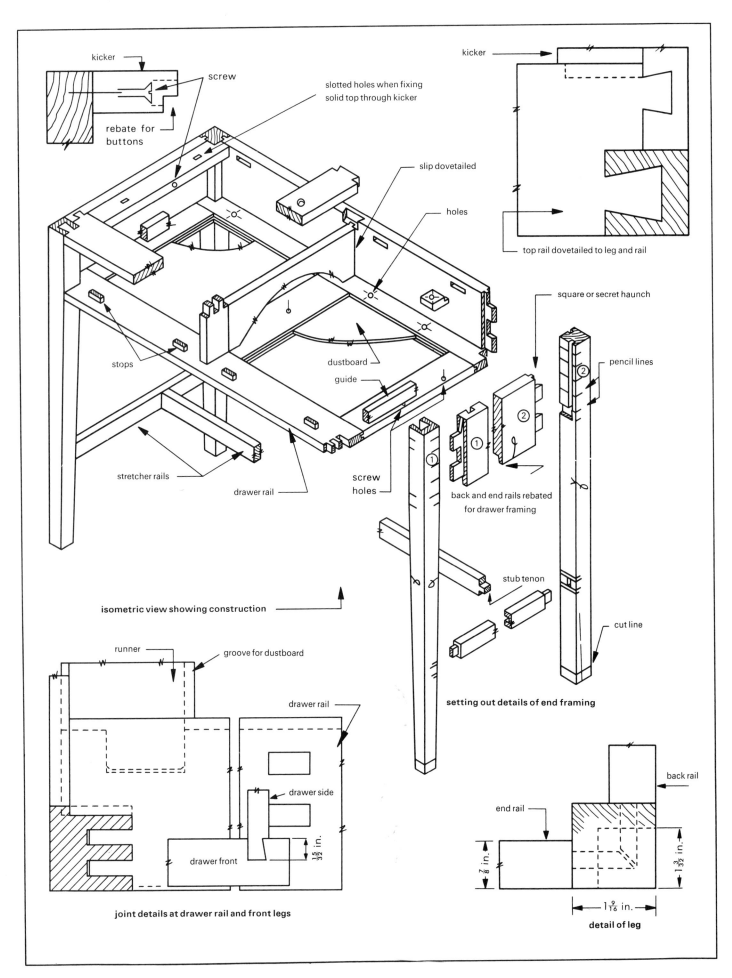

kicker

screw

rebate for buttons

slotted holes when fixing solid top through kicker

kicker

top rail dovetailed to leg and rail

slip dovetailed

holes

square or secret haunch

pencil lines

stops

dustboard

guide

back and end rails rebated for drawer framing

stub tenon

stretcher rails

drawer rail

screw holes

cut line

isometric view showing construction

setting out details of end framing

runner

groove for dustboard

drawer rail

drawer side

drawer front

$\frac{15}{32}$ in.

joint details at drawer rail and front legs

back rail

end rail

$\frac{7}{8}$ in.

$1\frac{3}{32}$ in.

$1\frac{9}{16}$ in.

detail of leg

72

Carcase construction

The drawings on page 74 give details of the setting-out of a common through dovetail joint on a carcase with an integral plinth. This arrangement is suitable for bookcases and small cupboards. Information on dovetail housing is also given.

Joints: Fig. 1 shows the method of setting-out the common dovetail joint. To the left and right of Fig. 1 are shown the pin arrangements necessary when making a mitred edge to cater for intersecting mouldings, rebated and ploughed-in backs, etc. See also mitred secret dovetail joint page 76 and pin arrangement for ploughed-in backs.

A gives an isometric view of a through dovetailed joint with the back pin arranged to accommodate a back which is to be rebated in.

Plain stopped and dovetail housing joints are also shown in the isometric views. The diminished dovetail housing joint is efficient and simple to make and owing to its taper obviously easy to assemble.

Housings for maximum strength should not enter the wood to a depth of more than $\frac{1}{3}$ of its thickness.

Note reinforcing angle blocks on plinth and bottom shelf or 'pot' board, and the use of buttons and fixing blocks. See also page 75.

Box Carcase Construction

Details of various joint arrangements suitable for box carcases in solid wood, ranging from small boxes to sideboards, etc., are shown on page 75. For use of laminboard in carcases see pages 86, 87, 89 and 90.

Joints: Fig. B page 75 shows an exploded view of lap dovetail joints and two simple methods of supporting adjustable shelving.

A secret or double lapped dovetail, and a dovetailed shouldered housing joint are shown at C.

Note alternative lap joint reinforced with keys and glue blocks, and method of securing plinth or tops to carcases. For setting-out mitred secret dovetail joint see pages 76 and 83.

Mitred secret dovetail joint

The drawings on page 76 give full details of the setting-out and making of this joint, see page 79 for technique of removing waste. Fig. 1 shows a buttressed rebate to take a panelled or laminboard back.

Note arrangement of pins to cater for rebate, and the various moulded edge treatments. Note also pin arrangements for the strengthening of wide carcases.

Exploded view of mitred secret dovetail.

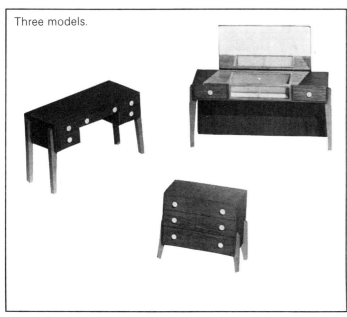

Three models.

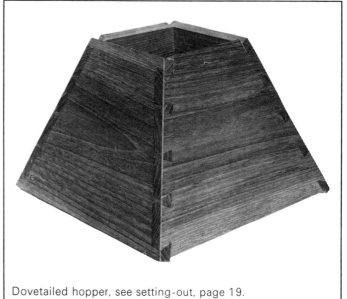

Dovetailed hopper, see setting-out, page 19.

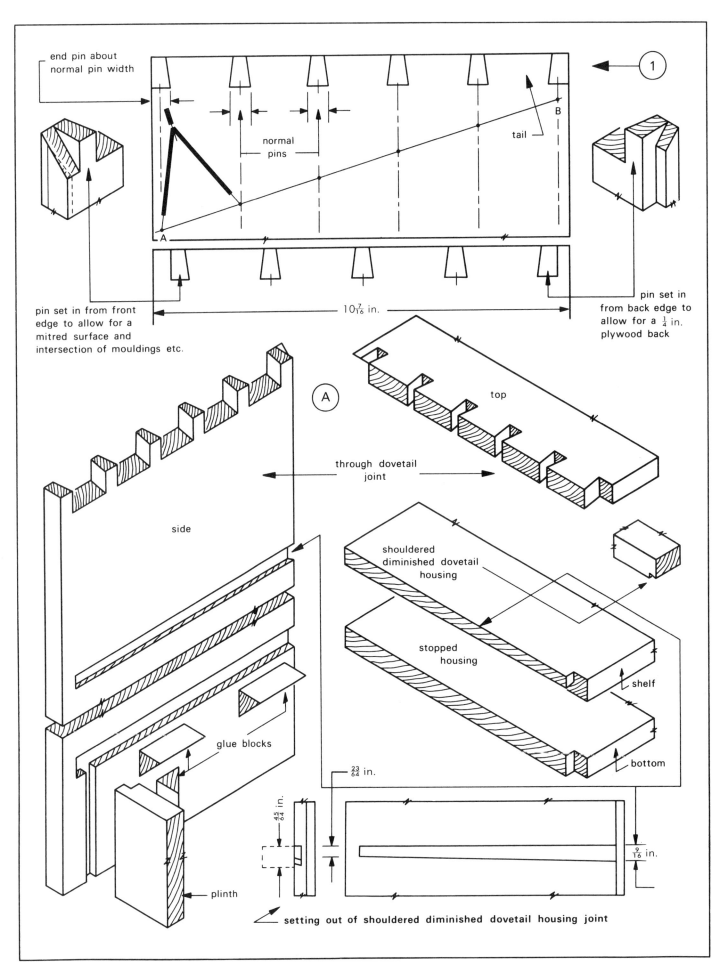

end pin about normal pin width

normal pins

tail

A

B

pin set in from front edge to allow for a mitred surface and intersection of mouldings etc.

pin set in from back edge to allow for a $\frac{1}{4}$ in. plywood back

$10\frac{7}{16}$ in.

1

A

through dovetail joint

side

top

shouldered diminished dovetail housing

stopped housing

shelf

bottom

glue blocks

plinth

$\frac{23}{64}$ in.

$\frac{45}{64}$ in.

$\frac{9}{16}$ in.

setting out of shouldered diminished dovetail housing joint

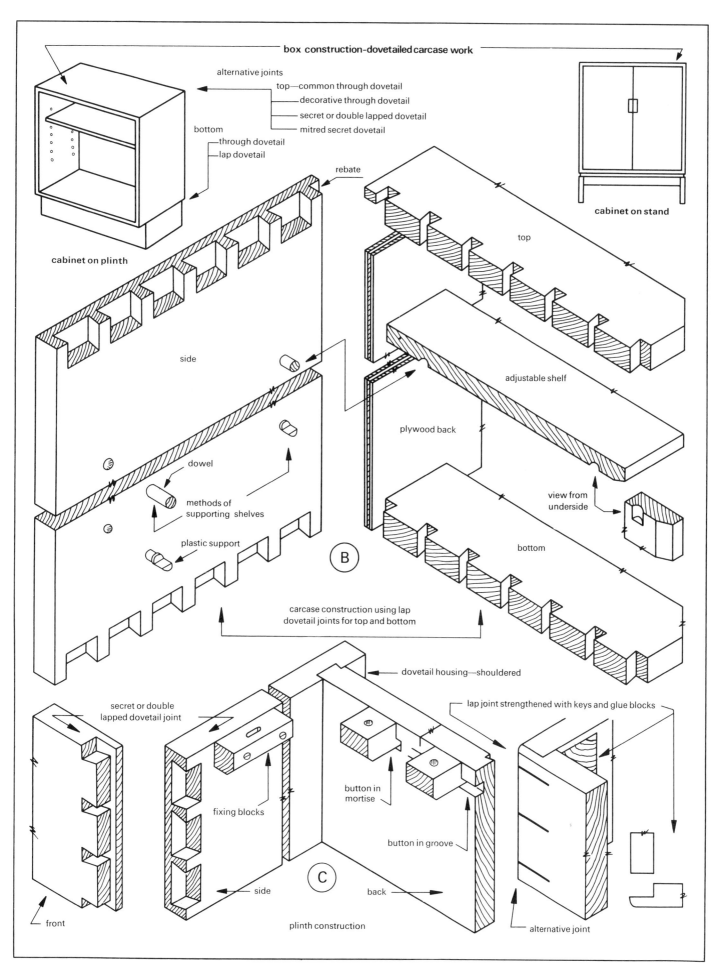

box construction-dovetailed carcase work

cabinet on stand

alternative joints

top—common through dovetail
decorative through dovetail
secret or double lapped dovetail
mitred secret dovetail

bottom
through dovetail
lap dovetail

cabinet on plinth

rebate

top

side

adjustable shelf

dowel

methods of
supporting shelves

plastic support

plywood back

view from
underside

bottom

B

carcase construction using lap
dovetail joints for top and bottom

dovetail housing—shouldered

secret or double
lapped dovetail joint

fixing blocks

button in
mortise

button in groove

lap joint strengthened with keys and glue blocks

side

back

front

C

plinth construction

alternative joint

75

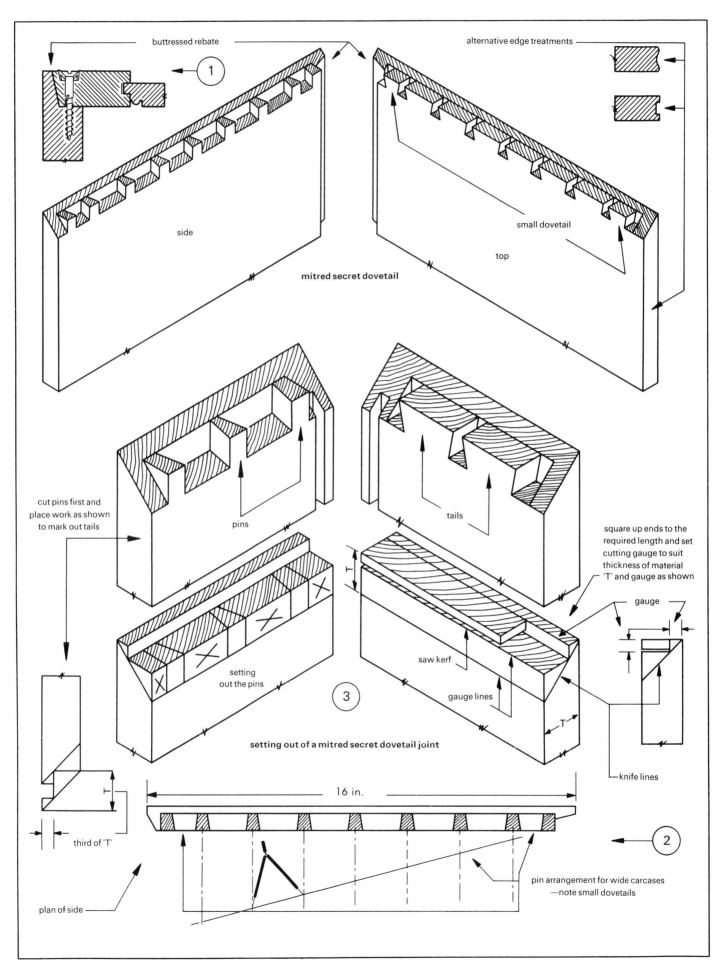

buttressed rebate

alternative edge treatments

①

side

top

mitred secret dovetail

small dovetail

cut pins first and
place work as shown
to mark out tails

pins

tails

square up ends to the
required length and set
cutting gauge to suit
thickness of material
'T' and gauge as shown

gauge

setting
out the pins

③

saw kerf

gauge lines

knife lines

setting out of a mitred secret dovetail joint

third of 'T'

16 in.

②

plan of side

pin arrangement for wide carcases
—note small dovetails

Drawer making and setting-out

Although the dovetailing machine has made it possible to mass produce drawers quickly, the craftsman's hand-made dovetail is still a sign of quality, and is much sought after. A high standard of craftsmanship is essential when making and fitting drawers.

The drawings on pages 78 and 79 give full information on the method of setting-out and making a drawer.

Fig. 1, page 78, shows one method of fitting drawer fronts and sides prior to marking out.

Fig. 2 is an isometric detail showing method of setting-out drawer.

Fig. 3 shows a technique of cutting dovetails. Note how one or more pairs of sides could be cut together.

Fig. 4 shows the method of marking out pins with tip of saw.

Fig. 5 shows the method of cutting pins.

Joints: Through dovetailing on drawer back. See drawer shown on page 67. Lap dovetailing on drawer fronts. Also see slip dovetail at drawer front page 90. The technique of marking out pins and tails with an awl is shown on page 79.

Fig. 6, page 79, shows the method of removing waste after cutting pins as illustrated in Fig. 5 page 78. See also use of coping saw to remove waste.

The sketch at Fig. 7 shows the joint in the process of assembly. Note how corners of the dovetails are eased to assist entry.

A method of making drawer slips by hand is shown on page 79. Note back views of two types of drawer slips.

Photograph showing bed, underbed storage unit and wall storage unit, 1,940mm (6ft 4½in) ×610mm (2ft) ×250mm (10in) with one sliding door, plastic laminate faced, the other upholstered. It is divided into two compartments with one adjustable shelf.
Photograph by courtesy of Gordon Russell.

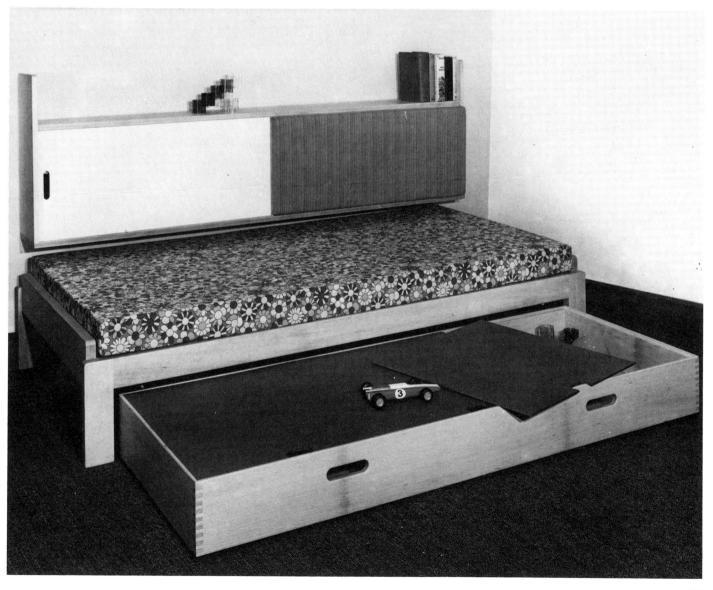

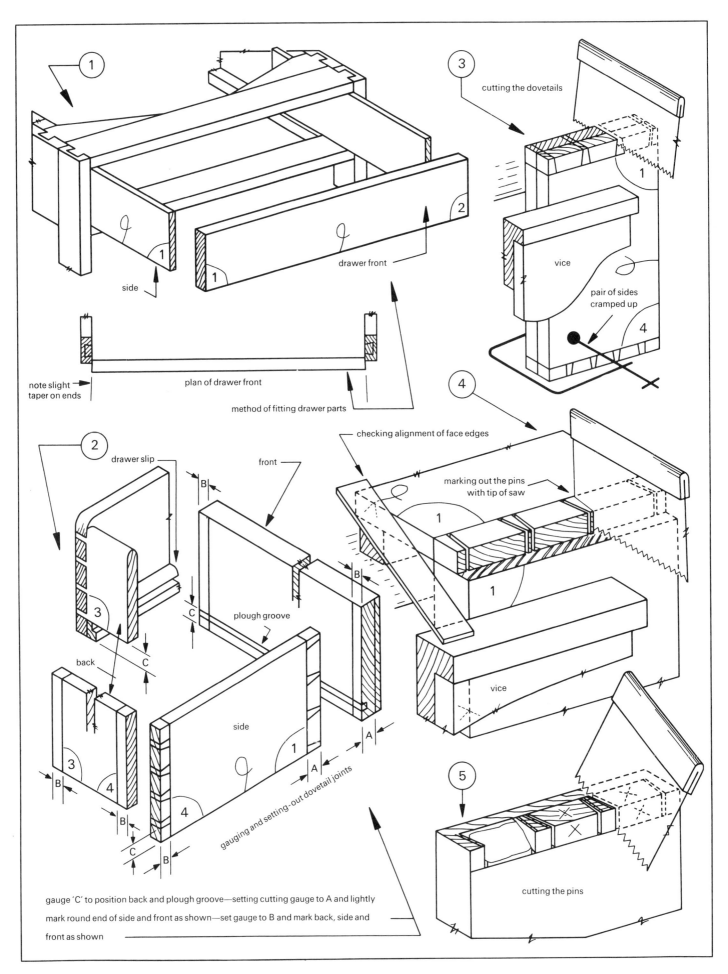

① side — drawer front

plan of drawer front

note slight taper on ends

method of fitting drawer parts

③ cutting the dovetails

vice

pair of sides cramped up

④ checking alignment of face edges

marking out the pins with tip of saw

vice

② drawer slip

front

plough groove

back

side

gauging and setting-out dovetail joints

⑤ cutting the pins

gauge 'C' to position back and plough groove—setting cutting gauge to A and lightly mark round end of side and front as shown—set gauge to B and mark back, side and front as shown

78

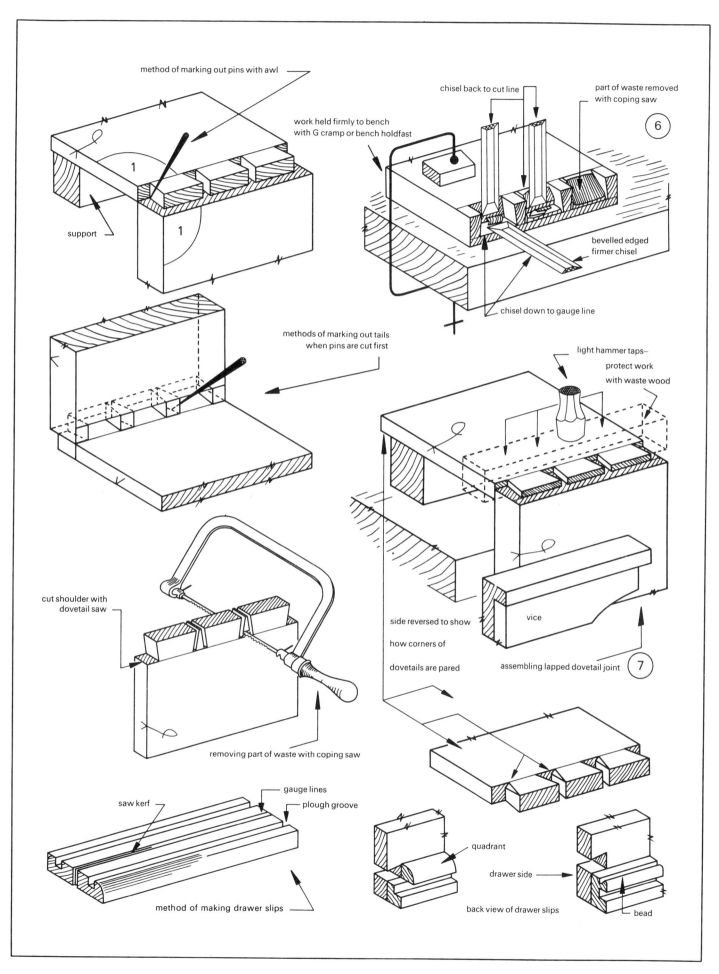

method of marking out pins with awl

work held firmly to bench with G cramp or bench holdfast

chisel back to cut line

part of waste removed with coping saw

6

support

1

1

bevelled edged firmer chisel

chisel down to gauge line

methods of marking out tails when pins are cut first

light hammer taps—
protect work
with waste wood

cut shoulder with dovetail saw

removing part of waste with coping saw

side reversed to show
how corners of
dovetails are pared

vice

assembling lapped dovetail joint

7

saw kerf

gauge lines

plough groove

quadrant

drawer side

method of making drawer slips

back view of drawer slips

bead

Box carcase construction

Wall bureau with drawer and stationery units
(See drawings page 81.)

Specification: The carcase is to be made in solid sapele, and lipped with projecting moulding of clear sycamore. The moulding is to be tongued and glued to the carcase, the mitred corners being reinforced with veneer keys of a similar wood.

The flap is to be made up of first quality laminboard and veneered in Nigerian pearwood, lipped with rosewood.

The lipping is to stand proud of the surface – see enlarged detail.

The inside of the flap is to incorporate a writing surface of leather, the outer edges of which are to be decorated with an embossed gold border pattern.

The flap is to be hung with centre hinges, and is to be self-supporting as shown in section BB.

All interior fittings to be in prime quality white sycamore.

Handles for drawers are to be made in rosewood.

The back may be in plywood and veneered to match the carcase.

Finish: interior is to be polished lightly with white French polish;
exterior is to be white French polished, to an eggshell or matt finish.

The working drawings on page 81 coupled with the above specification give all the necessary information that a craftsman would need to make the bureau.

The drawings show:
1 An elevation with flap down.
2 Plan and section 'AA'.
3 A vertical section 'BB'.
4 Enlarged detail of moulding and flap.

Joints: Main carcase; mitred secret dovetail; carcase for drawer and stationery units; through dovetails and stopped housing, all with mitred intersections.

Cutting list

Carcase

	Length	Width	Thickness	Material
1 bottom	$26\frac{3}{4}$ in.	$8\frac{1}{2}$ in.	$\frac{3}{4}$ in.	sapele
1 top	$26\frac{3}{4}$ in.	$6\frac{11}{16}$ in.	$\frac{3}{4}$ in.	sapele
2 ends	$16\frac{3}{4}$ in.	$8\frac{1}{2}$ in.	$\frac{3}{4}$ in.	sapele
2 for edge mouldings	$27\frac{5}{32}$ in.	1 in.	$\frac{7}{8}$ in.	sycamore
2 for edge mouldings	$17\frac{1}{8}$ in.	1 in.	$\frac{7}{8}$ in.	sycamore
1 back	$26\frac{3}{8}$ in.	$16\frac{1}{2}$ in.	$\frac{3}{16}$ in.	plywood faced sycamore

	Length	Width	Thickness	Material
1 flap	$26\frac{3}{16}$ in.	$15\frac{3}{4}$ in.	$\frac{11}{16}$ in.	laminboard
2 pieces	$16\frac{1}{8}$ in.	$26\frac{3}{8}$ in.	double	knife-cut veneer as specified
2 pieces of lipping	$26\frac{3}{16}$ in.	$\frac{15}{16}$ in.	$\frac{1}{2}$ in.	rosewood
2 pieces of lipping	$16\frac{1}{8}$ in.	$\frac{15}{16}$ in.	$\frac{1}{2}$ in.	rosewood

1 small oddment for handles in rosewood

Interior Units

	Length	Width	Thickness	Material
3 pieces, top, bottom and division for drawer unit	$25\frac{9}{16}$ in.	6 in.	$\frac{1}{4}$ in.	sycamore
3 pieces, vertical members for drawer unit	$5\frac{1}{2}$ in.	6 in.	$\frac{1}{4}$ in.	sycamore
1 drawer front	$7\frac{1}{16}$ in.	$2\frac{9}{16}$ in.	$\frac{1}{2}$ in.	sycamore
1 drawer front	$7\frac{1}{16}$ in.	$2\frac{3}{16}$ in.	$\frac{1}{2}$ in.	sycamore
2 sides	6 in.	$2\frac{9}{16}$ in.	$\frac{3}{16}$ in.	sycamore
2 sides	6 in.	$2\frac{3}{16}$ in.	$\frac{3}{16}$ in.	sycamore
1 back	$7\frac{1}{16}$ in.	$2\frac{9}{16}$ in.	$\frac{3}{16}$ in.	sycamore
1 back	$7\frac{1}{16}$ in.	$2\frac{3}{16}$ in.	$\frac{3}{16}$ in.	sycamore
2 bottoms	$7\frac{1}{16}$ in.	6 in.	$\frac{3}{16}$ in.	plywood

Lower Unit

	Length	Width	Thickness	Material
1 back	$17\frac{11}{16}$ in.	4 in.	$\frac{1}{4}$ in.	sycamore
1 middle	$17\frac{11}{16}$ in.	$3\frac{7}{16}$ in.	$\frac{1}{4}$ in.	sycamore
1 front	$17\frac{11}{16}$ in.	3 in.	$\frac{1}{4}$ in.	sycamore
2 ends	$4\frac{3}{4}$ in.	4 in.	$\frac{1}{4}$ in.	sycamore
1 to cut 2 divisions	$4\frac{3}{4}$ in.	4 in.	$\frac{1}{4}$ in.	sycamore
1 bottom	$17\frac{11}{16}$ in.	$4\frac{3}{4}$ in.	$\frac{3}{16}$ in.	plywood

1 piece of leather as required for flap

1 cut cupboard lock and escutcheon

1 pair of centre hinges and screws

16 15mm ($\frac{5}{8}$ in.) x No. 6 brass screws and cups for back

4 brass mirror plates and screws

Right:
Wall bureau designed and made by the author, 1952.

Interior, showing sycamore drawer units. The lower unit has been arranged to slide and it can also be easily removed.

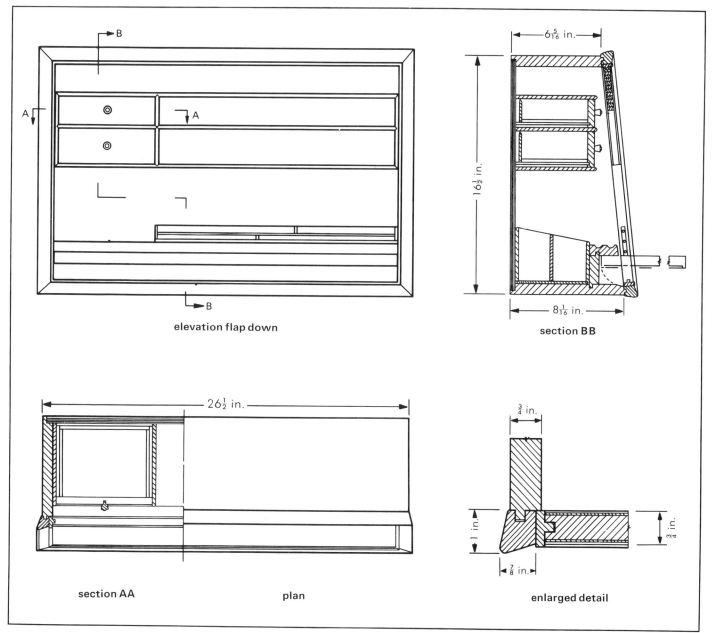

elevation flap down

section BB

section AA

plan

enlarged detail

Presentation boxes or caskets

Boxes of this nature offer considerable scope for originality in design, and an opportunity for the craftsman to produce work of the highest quality. These boxes can be made in an infinite variety of shapes, and in many kinds of woods. They can also incorporate trays when designed for jewellery. They may be decorated with mouldings, and carving, inlays of contrasting wood, metal and ivory, etc. A selection of designs is shown below and on pages 83 and 84. The drawings below show a plan, elevation and sections of a casket, and an exploded view of a secret or double lapped dovetail joint. The lid is decorated with a cavetto moulding which is worked on the solid. The lid is hinged in a vee groove and arranged so that it rests — when open — in a near vertical position. The plinth is mitred, dowelled and glued to the base.

Note: rebates to receive top and bottom veneered plywood, and the location of linings.

Joints: double lapped dovetail, with pins arranged to allow for sawing off the lid. Note arrangement of joint to cater for mitred edges to closing surfaces of box and lid.

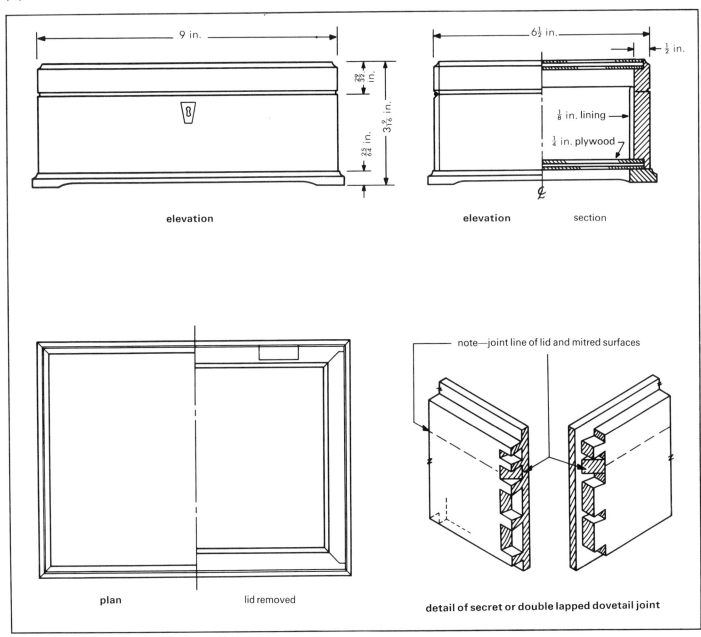

elevation

elevation   section

plan   lid removed

detail of secret or double lapped dovetail joint

Oak casket. Shaped plinth and lipping in laburnum.
Designed and made by the author, 1956.

Oak casket with lid open.

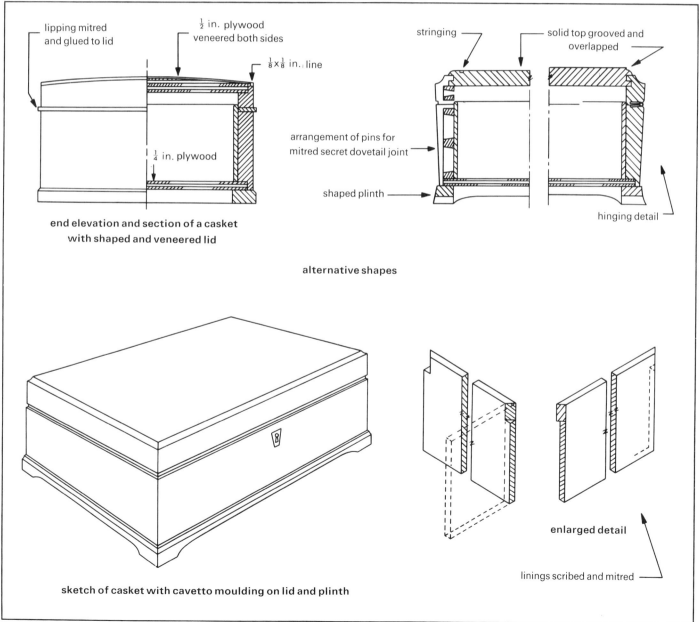

lipping mitred
and glued to lid

$\frac{1}{2}$ in. plywood
veneered both sides

$\frac{1}{8} \times \frac{1}{8}$ in. line

$\frac{1}{4}$ in. plywood

**end elevation and section of a casket
with shaped and veneered lid**

stringing

solid top grooved and
overlapped

arrangement of pins for
mitred secret dovetail joint

shaped plinth

hinging detail

alternative shapes

sketch of casket with cavetto moulding on lid and plinth

enlarged detail

linings scribed and mitred

Design for caskets

The drawings on page 83 show a perspective sketch of the previous casket, and two other designs, incorporating multi-ply and solid wood tops respectively. One design shows a box with a shaped lid made up of multi-ply and veneered. The second design shows in section details of alternative solid tops, that on the right is moulded, and to the left is shown a solid top with a small quadrant worked on the top edge. It is further decorated with a contrasting inlay.

Note technique of making up lids, and provision to allow for possible shrinkage. Generally this kind of top should not be glued in.

Joints: Mitred secret dovetail, note arrangement of pins to cater for sawn off lid. An enlarged detail gives particulars of scribed and mitred linings as fitted to the interior of box. See page 76 for mitred secret dovetail joint.

Mahogany casket with boxwood lines. Designed and made by the author, 1970.

Yew casket with shaped sides and top. Designed and made by the author, 1969.

Yew casket with lid open showing walnut lining.

Box construction

(Using mainly laminboard or blockboard as a main carcase material.) The constructional technique outlined in pages 86, 87, 89 and 90 can be equally well applied to other articles of furniture, such as wardrobes, cupboards, cocktail cabinets, wall units, etc. A pictorial sketch of a sideboard with sunk handles is shown in Fig. 1, page 86. The carcase is supported on a stool or stand.

Constructional details and a method of making up and securing a veneered laminboard top are also shown in Fig. 1.

The design shown in Fig. 2 page 86 is for a small sideboard which is to be fitted with flush doors and drawers, and supported on a full length stool. The drawers are supported on runners housed into the carcase; all drawer framing is omitted.

Special features and suggestions: Note the rebate worked on the top of the stool in Fig. 2; this makes a pleasing feature and a clean break between the stool and carcase.

The constructional details given in Fig. 2 show an interesting method of securing bottom to carcase. The veneered lamin or blockboard bottom is glued and screwed to the rails, and the divisions can be suitably housed in. The thickness of the bottom makes adequate door and drawer stops.

Handles: For the sideboard, Fig. 1, the drawers are to be fitted with neat handles of a contrasting wood. The sliding doors are to have sunk handles, with a background to match the drawer handles. For sideboard, Fig. 2, the handles are in aluminium (all edges softened) and are to be matt brushed finished.

Joints: Note: divisions are tenoned into top rails. The top and bottom rails of carcases, Fig. 2, are lap dovetailed to the laminboard ends.

The bottom of the sideboard illustrated in Fig. 1 may be lap dovetailed, dowelled or tongued and grooved. See also enlarged details on page 75.

At Fig. 3, enlarged details are given showing the jointing of top rails into the laminboard and the 'housing in' of drawer runners.

Model furniture in mahogany and sycamore. Scale: 1 in = 1 ft.

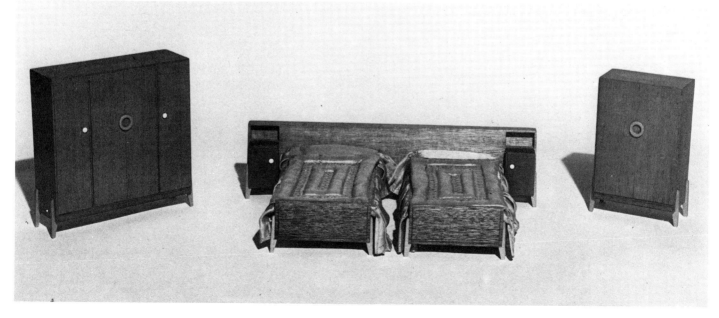

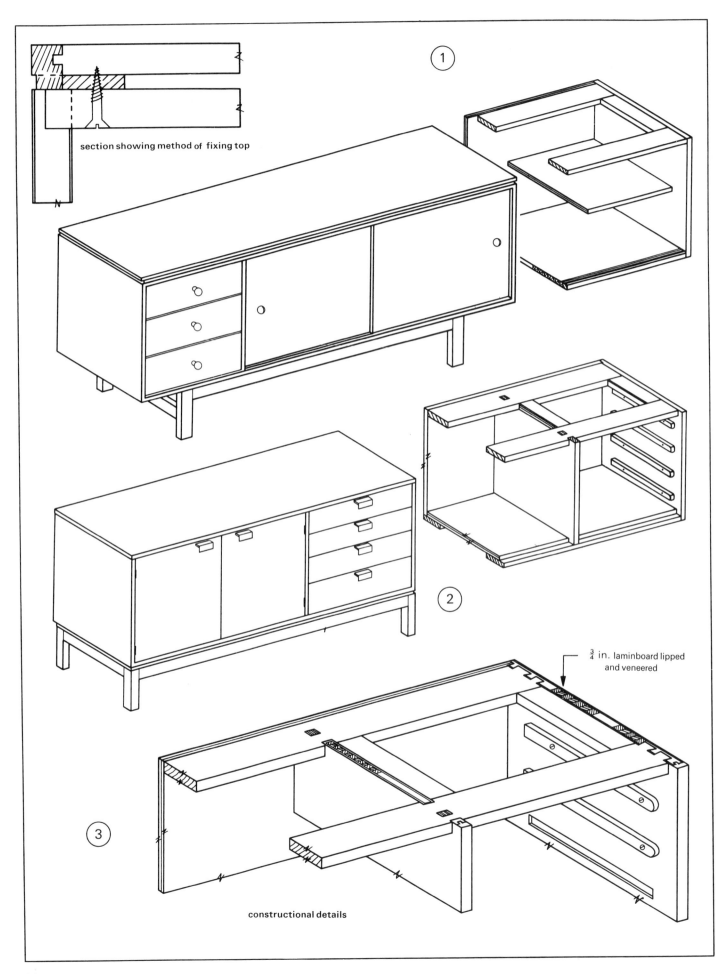

section showing method of fixing top

①

②

¾ in. laminboard lipped
and veneered

③

constructional details

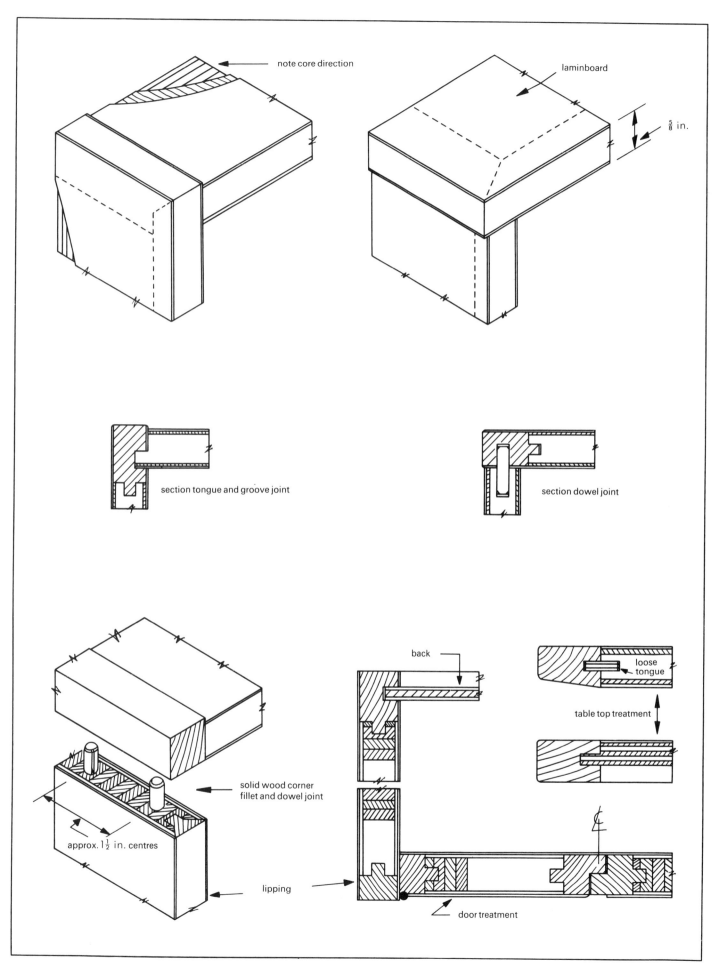

note core direction

laminboard

$\frac{5}{8}$ in.

section tongue and groove joint

section dowel joint

solid wood corner
fillet and dowel joint

approx. $1\frac{1}{2}$ in. centres

lipping

back

loose
tongue

table top treatment

door treatment

87

Sideboard with laminboard ends

The main features of the sideboard illustrated on page 89 are:

1 The integral carcase ends. These ends extend to floor line to give support, and dispense with the necessity of having a stool or stand.

2 The doors are designed to hang outside the carcase and the drawers are arranged to match.

Full working drawings are shown, these consist of an elevation, a plan with the top removed, and two vertical sections 'AA' and 'BB'.

Also shown is an isometric view giving details of the interior and construction; note the enlarged details showing proportions of joints and lipping. The lipping on the opening edges of the doors is moulded to form a convenient grip for opening and closing.

Further drawings of the sideboard are given on page 90 They consist of an exploded isometric view, showing all the main joints, and enlarged details of a drawer and door. A cutting list is given below.

Section 'AA' gives hinging and drawer details; note the slip dovetailing at drawer fronts. The method of fitting the bottom to the carcase ends is clearly shown. The bottom is housed in and glued, and is securely fixed to the ends by means of solid wood fillets and screws.

The drawings on page 87 show various jointing techniques suitable for carcases made in manufactured board.

Cutting list
Carcase

Description	Length	Width	Thickness	Material
2 sides	$29\frac{1}{2}$ in.	$16\frac{1}{2}$ in.	$\frac{11}{16}$ in.	laminboard
1 top	63 in.	$16\frac{1}{2}$ in.	$\frac{11}{16}$ in.	laminboard
1 bottom	63 in.	$16\frac{1}{2}$ in.	$\frac{11}{16}$ in.	laminboard
2 divisions	$21\frac{5}{8}$ in.	$15\frac{3}{4}$ in.	$\frac{11}{16}$ in.	laminboard
2 top rails	63 in.	$2\frac{3}{8}$ in.	$\frac{3}{4}$ in.	hardwood
2 supporting rails for bottom	63 in.	$1\frac{3}{4}$ in.	$\frac{7}{8}$ in.	hardwood
2 fillets	$13\frac{3}{4}$ in.	$1\frac{3}{8}$ in.	$1\frac{3}{8}$ in.	beech
2 vertical rails	$20\frac{7}{8}$ in.	$1\frac{3}{4}$ in.	$\frac{3}{4}$ in.	hardwood
2 drawer rails	$22\frac{7}{16}$ in.	1 in.	$\frac{3}{4}$ in.	hardwood
4 runners	15 in.	1 in.	$\frac{3}{4}$ in.	hardwood
1 back	63 in.	$21\frac{5}{8}$ in.	$\frac{3}{8}$ in.	plywood
3 drawer fronts	22 in.	$7\frac{1}{16}$ in.	$\frac{3}{4}$ in.	hardwood
6 drawer sides	$15\frac{3}{4}$ in.	$6\frac{11}{16}$ in.	$\frac{3}{8}$ in.	hardwood
3 drawer backs	22 in.	$6\frac{5}{16}$ in.	$\frac{3}{8}$ in.	hardwood
3 drawer bottoms	$21\frac{5}{8}$ in.	$15\frac{3}{4}$ in.	$\frac{1}{4}$ in.	plywood
6 plough slips	$15\frac{3}{4}$ in.	$\frac{7}{8}$ in.	$\frac{1}{2}$ in.	hardwood

Lipping for ends as required
Plywood for loose tongues as required

Doors

Description	Length	Width	Thickness	Material
2 doors	$21\frac{5}{8}$ in.	$20\frac{11}{16}$ in.	$\frac{11}{16}$ in.	laminboard
4 lippings	$42\frac{5}{16}$ in.	$\frac{7}{8}$ in.	$\frac{11}{16}$ in.	hardwood
2 shelves	$20\frac{11}{16}$ in.	$15\frac{3}{4}$ in.	$\frac{3}{8}$ in.	plywood to be veneered and lipped on front edge.

Veneers for carcase and doors, order as required
2 pairs of 2 in. solid brass butts and screws.
1 pair of magnetic catches
Screws and cups for fixing back as needed

When making up cutting lists for carcase and door work which is required to be made in laminboard or blockboard, it is essential to arrange for the 'core' to run in the direction which will give the maximum strength.

Model making

Model furniture showing a complete bedroom suite. The chest of drawers, writing and dressing tables are made of solid wood. Legs are in sycamore, and these are glued and secretly pinned to the carcase. The small plastic handles are made from knitting needles, and are fixed with glue and small panel pins.
Carcases for the lady's and gentleman's wardrobes are made up from 9mm ($\frac{3}{8}$in) thick mahogany. The continental type of headboard, small cabinets and bed framing, are also made out of solid wood. Model furniture scale: 1in. = 1ft. Designed and made by the author.

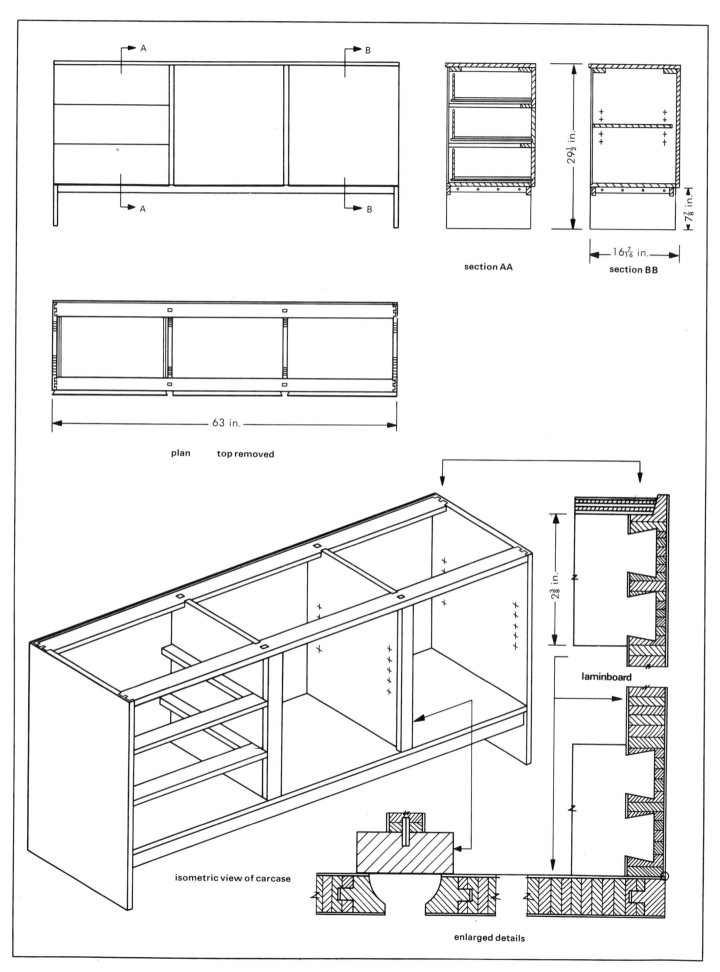

section AA

section BB

$29\frac{1}{2}$ in.

$7\frac{7}{8}$ in.

$16\frac{7}{16}$ in.

63 in.

plan   top removed

$2\frac{3}{8}$ in.

laminboard

isometric view of carcase

enlarged details

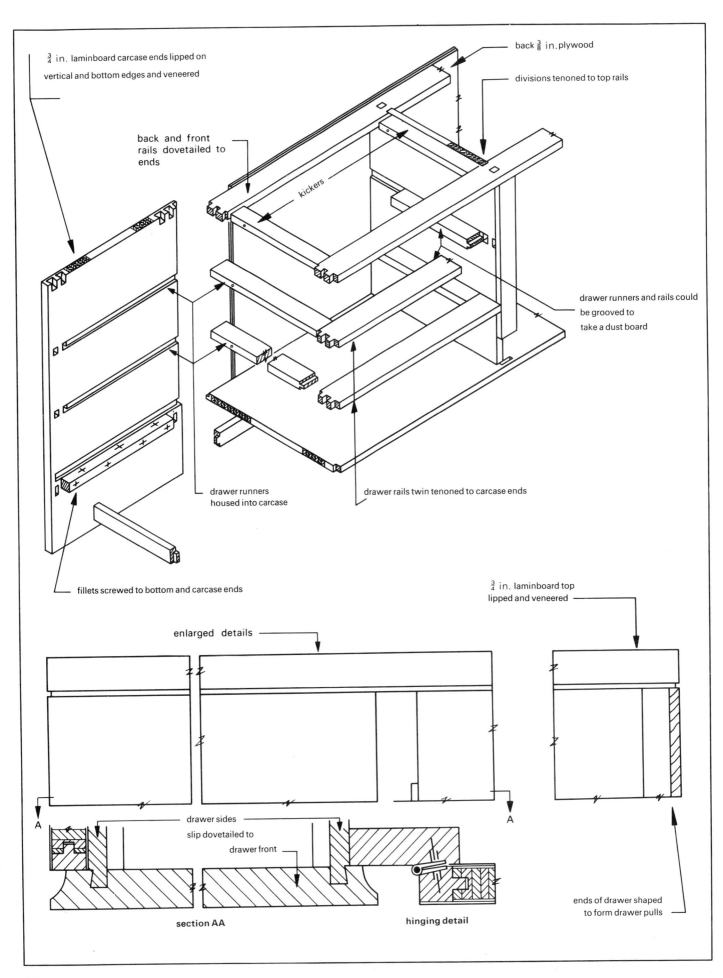

¾ in. laminboard carcase ends lipped on
vertical and bottom edges and veneered

back ⅜ in. plywood

divisions tenoned to top rails

back and front
rails dovetailed to
ends

kickers

drawer runners and rails could
be grooved to
take a dust board

drawer runners
housed into carcase

drawer rails twin tenoned to carcase ends

fillets screwed to bottom and carcase ends

¾ in. laminboard top
lipped and veneered

enlarged details

A

A

drawer sides
slip dovetailed to
drawer front

section AA

hinging detail

ends of drawer shaped
to form drawer pulls

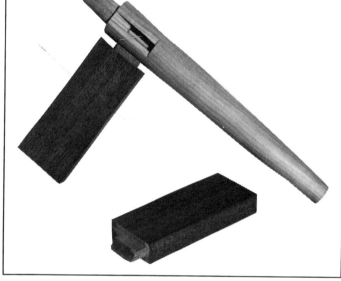

Top:
Balsa model of dining chair with framed back.

Below:
Model of easy chair in balsa wood.
Very few tools are required for model-making in balsa wood.
The following should be quite adequate: steel rule, small
try-square, dovetail saw, Stanley knife, 25mm (1in) paring
chisel, small fine flat and round files, block plane, sandpaper,
adhesive – balsa cement.

Top:
Balsa model of dining chair with two back rails.

Below:
Joints between turned legs and rail, suitable for chair and table
construction. The shoulders of the joint shown on the left are
scribed over the legs. The shoulders of the rail – bottom of
picture – are left square, but a portion below the tenon is
scribed over the leg to counteract possible shrinkage.
Note portion of leg removed to form seating.

Various techniques and construction

The following pages 91–95 give useful information on
various techniques and construction, dealing with
chairs, semi-circular and circular table work, also the
problems involved in barred door work, and the method
of setting out a knuckle joint for brackets to support a
drop leaf type of table.

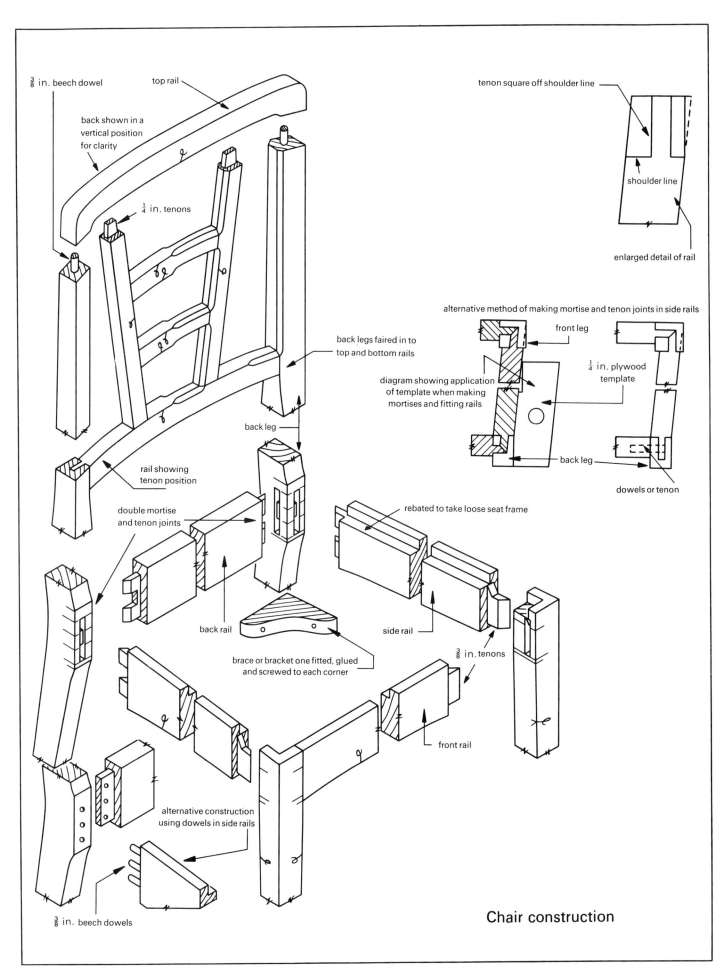

$\frac{3}{8}$ in. beech dowel

top rail

back shown in a vertical position for clarity

$\frac{1}{4}$ in. tenons

tenon square off shoulder line

shoulder line

enlarged detail of rail

back legs faired in to top and bottom rails

back leg

alternative method of making mortise and tenon joints in side rails

front leg

diagram showing application of template when making mortises and fitting rails

$\frac{1}{4}$ in. plywood template

back leg

dowels or tenon

rail showing tenon position

double mortise and tenon joints

rebated to take loose seat frame

back rail

side rail

brace or bracket one fitted, glued and screwed to each corner

$\frac{3}{8}$ in. tenons

front rail

alternative construction using dowels in side rails

$\frac{3}{8}$ in. beech dowels

Chair construction

Semi-circular table. Top removed showing dovetail joints between laminated shaped rail and back legs, the bridle joint at front leg and buttons for fixing top. See working drawing page 28.

Small circular table with top removed.
The rim is built up of four pieces of 4mm ($\frac{3}{16}$in) plywood with grain of outer plies running vertically.
For a circular dining table the rim could be made up with beech constructional veneers to a thickness of approximately 21mm ($\frac{7}{8}$in) to suit dimensions and stability of table.

Table brackets with knuckle joints.
The bracket in the foreground has a knuckle joint which allows the bracket to open in two directions.
The top bracket is made to open in one position only as shown. These brackets are very strong and will give a life time of service. Besides being used for supporting flaps, they may be tenoned into legs which are designed to move and support table tops. See also drawing on page 94.

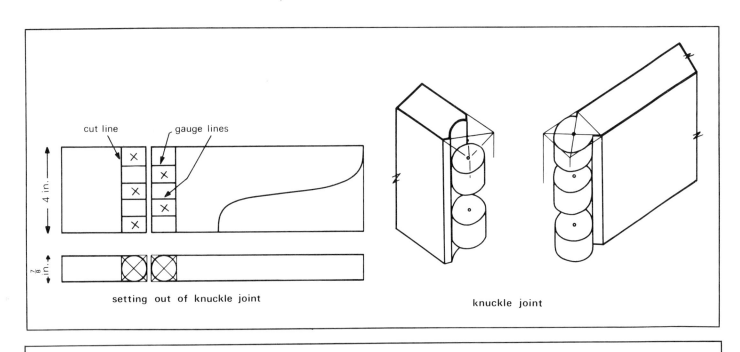

cut line

gauge lines

4 in.

$\frac{7}{8}$ in.

setting out of knuckle joint

knuckle joint

Barred door, with astragal mouldings, showing slats and dovetail joint in the foreground.
The drawing shown opposite gives details of construction.

Second view of barred door showing slats assembled.

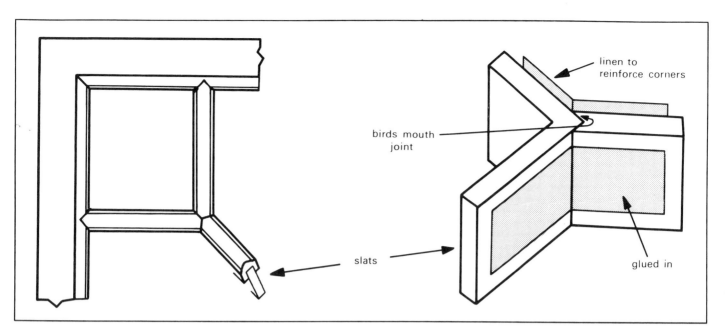

linen to
reinforce corners

birds mouth
joint

glued in

slats

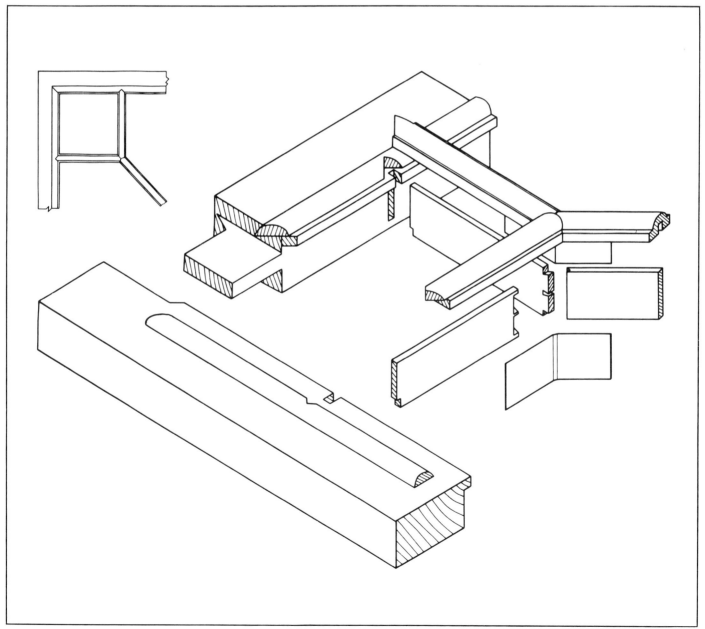

Perspective drawing

Perspective drawing is a highly technical subject; it requires much study and practice to become really efficient in the art. A number of methods are adopted to produce simple practical solutions, and these can be quite satisfactory for general purposes.

Perspective sketching is useful when presenting or developing a design, or preparing sketches for clients. As one becomes familiar with the techniques, much of the constructional work can be omitted.

The perspective drawings shown here are of an elementary nature, but the basic principles outlined should enable the student to practise simple perspective.

The drawings have been arranged so that the constructional techniques can be easily followed. The numbered procedure notes, coupled with a corresponding numbered drawing,will, I hope, be of some assistance to students of design, and to craftsmen.

The objects in the perspective drawings on pages 97, 98 and 99 are all shown inclined to the 'picture plane', and the drawings are made in what is known as 'angular perspective.'

Sideboard in angular perspective

To make a perspective drawing of the sideboard shown on page 97.
1 Draw the necessary plan and elevation required for dimensioning and main details.
2 Draw a horizontal line to represent the **picture plane**
3 Select a suitable angle to give the views required and draw the **plan** making one corner touching the picture plane. Note section giving heights and measuring line.
4 Project a vertical line from a point where the plan touches the picture plane. This is known as the **central ray of vision (C.R.V.)**. On this line mark off the distance the observer is standing from the picture plane (P.P.). This is known as the **station point** (S.P.).Care is needed in fixing this point, as the nearer we are to the

P.P. the greater the distortion. The drawings on pages 97 and 98 give varying distances for the S.P. These have been arranged – in some cases – to contain the **vanishing points** (V.P.) within the drawing, and to give as much information as possible with the limited space available; the drawings make this quite clear.
5 From the S.P. draw lines parallel with the front and side of the object shown in plan; these two lines make an angle of 90° and extend to the picture plane. The point of intersection of these two lines with the P.P. are known as vanishing points (V.P.).
Draw lines radiating from S.P. to major points on the plan, see drawings pages 97 and 98.
6 Select a convenient position for a base or ground line. This can, of course, vary according to the space available. The perspective drawings of the sideboard and chair shown on pages 97 and 98 are both drawn below the S.P. mainly to avoid superimposing work over construction lines, while the writing table shown on page 99 is contained above the S.P.
7 Draw eye or horizontal line about 1500mm (5ft) above ground line. This is considered a convenient height to represent eye level. This measurement is often reduced to obtain better views, and is largely governed by the height of article and views required.
8 Extend C.R.V. or vertical line – from where the plan of object touches picture plane – to locate ground line. On this vertical line, mark off the main heights taken from the elevation. See measuring line shown in drawing page 97.
9 To locate the V.P. on the eye line, simply project from the V.P. locations on the P.P. down to the eye line. From the measuring line giving height of object, draw lines converging to V.P.s situated on eye level.
10 The perspective length and depth of the object and other vertical details are obtained by dropping perpendiculars from the intersections made by the construction lines – within the **cone of vision** – and the picture plane.

See drawing page 97. Fig. 1, page 99, shows a diagramatic perspective layout for a wardrobe which is above eye level.

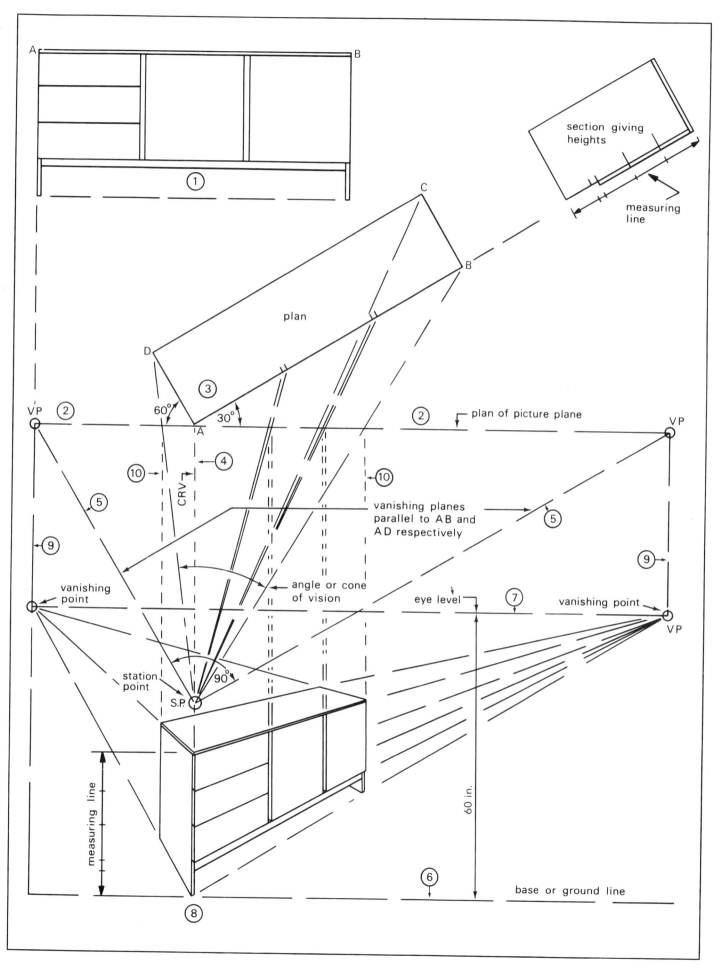

A ┌─────────────────────┐ B
①

section giving heights

measuring line

C

plan

B

D

③

VP ②

60°   30°

A

plan of picture plane

②

VP

⑩   ④   ⑩

CRV

⑤

vanishing planes parallel to AB and AD respectively

⑤

⑨

⑨

vanishing point

angle or cone of vision

eye level ⑦

vanishing point

VP

station point

90°

S.P.

measuring line

60 in.

⑥

base or ground line

⑧

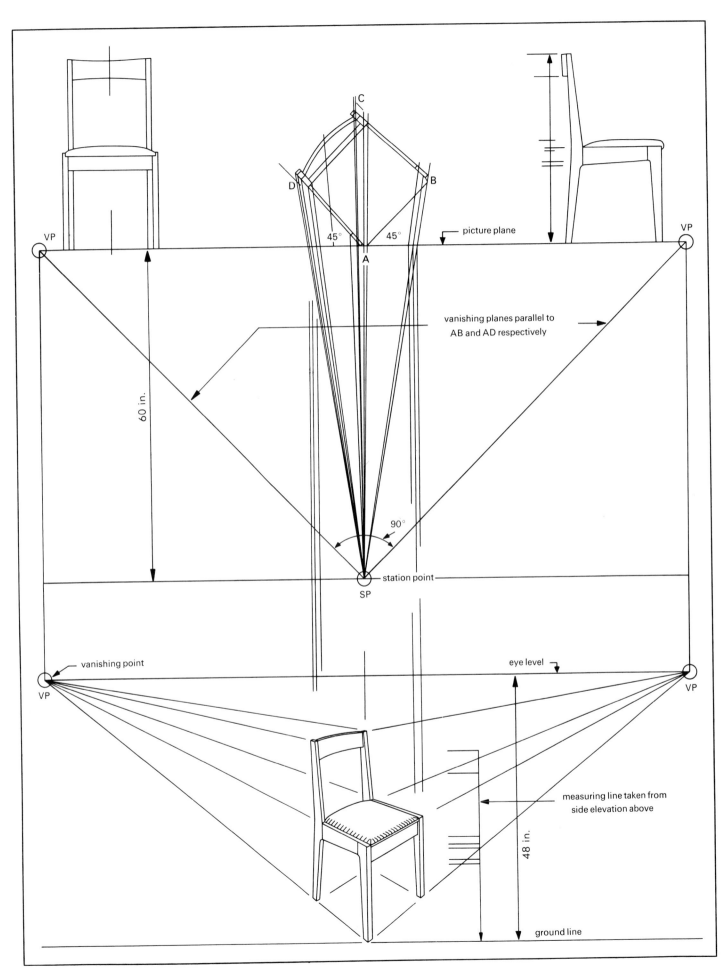

picture plane

C

D · · B

45° · 45°

A

vanishing planes parallel to
AB and AD respectively

VP

60 in.

90°

station point
SP

vanishing point

eye level

VP

VP

measuring line taken from
side elevation above

48 in.

ground line

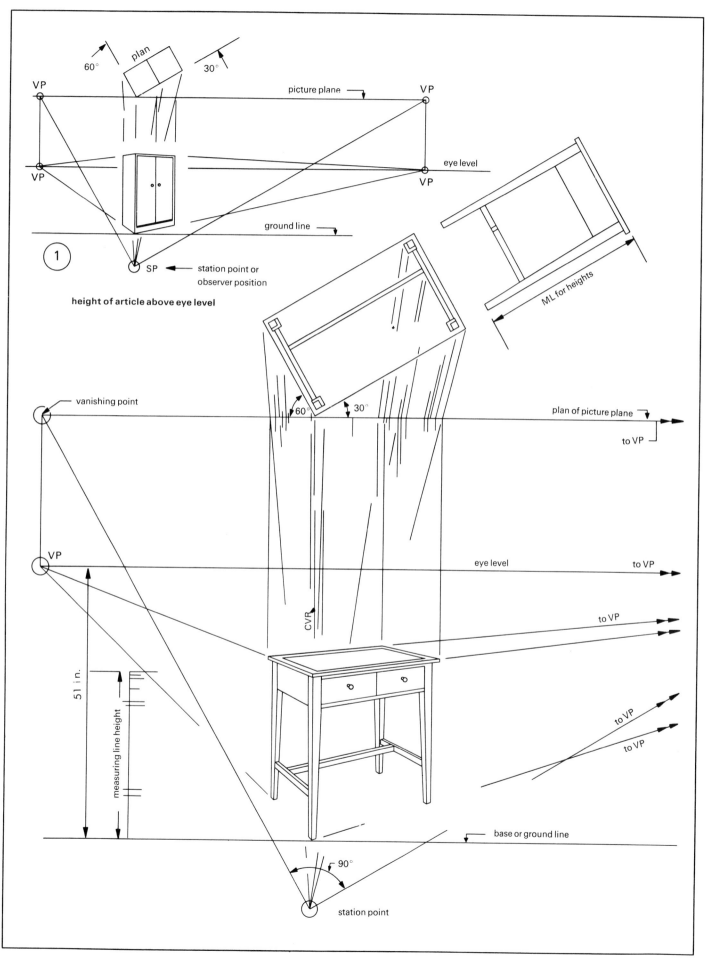

plan

60°   30°

VP   picture plane   VP

eye level

VP   VP

ground line

① SP ← station point or observer position

height of article above eye level

ML for heights

vanishing point

60°   30°   plan of picture plane

to VP

VP   eye level   to VP

CVR   to VP

51 in.

measuring line height   to VP
                                               to VP

base or ground line

90°

station point

99

Parallel perspective

Parallel perspective is a convenient and simple method of drawing interiors showing articles of furniture, etc. The drawing of an interior is shown on page 101, and the necessary procedure for constructing this is as follows. Select a suitable point at eye level in your picture, C.R.V. shown here as V.P. This is the central ray of vision. Extend the C.R.V. as shown and on this line fix a station point so that the angle of vision — 60° — is conveniently placed. Vanishing planes are drawn to meet the P.P. as shown previously. These planes are now **measuring vanishing points** (M.V.P.). Measuring points are located from the plan showing wall units 'A', and part plan of room. These points are now joined with M.V.P.1 on the eye level 1500mm (5ft) above ground line, and they give all the necessary location points for the width of the article. Measuring points at 'B' give location of settee and entrance door; these are shown at B. Join these points to M.V.P.2.

The method of application of measuring points for heights of objects is clearly shown on the right of the interior. These heights are connected to the C.R.V. shown here in the window.

Change of view can be arranged by re-positioning the C.R.V.

Teenage room: 2,900mm (9ft 6in) run of Tapley S.L. Wall System.
Layout to Heal's specification.
Photograph by courtesy of Heal and Son Ltd.

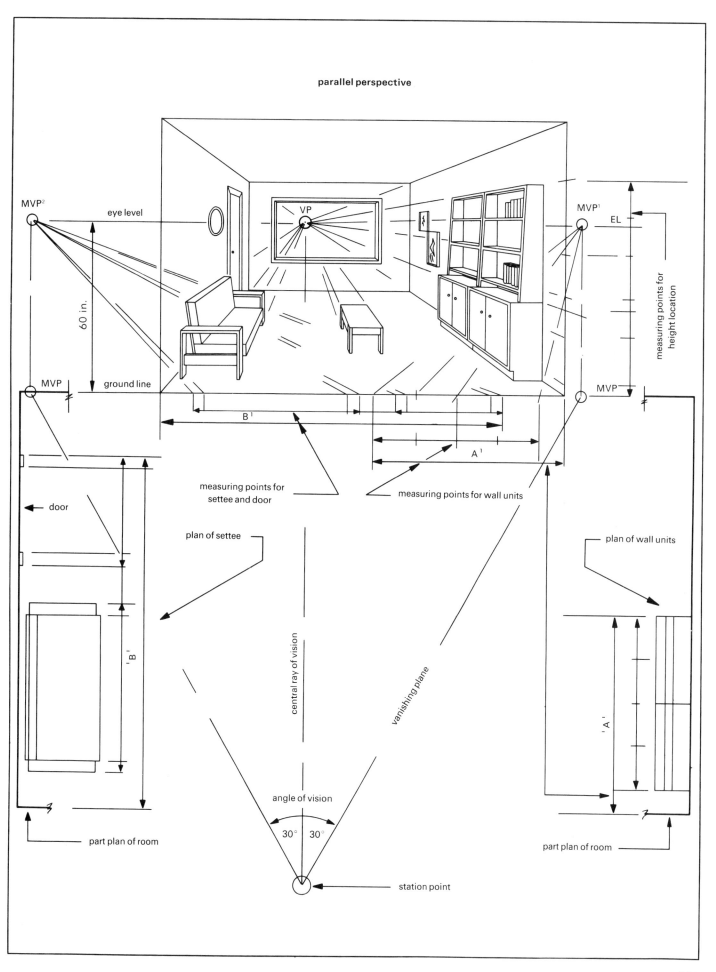

parallel perspective

MVP²

eye level

VP

MVP¹

EL

60 in.

measuring points for height location

MVP

ground line

MVP

B¹

A¹

measuring points for settee and door

measuring points for wall units

plan of settee

plan of wall units

door

'B'

'A'

central ray of vision

vanishing plane

part plan of room

part plan of room

angle of vision

30°   30°

station point

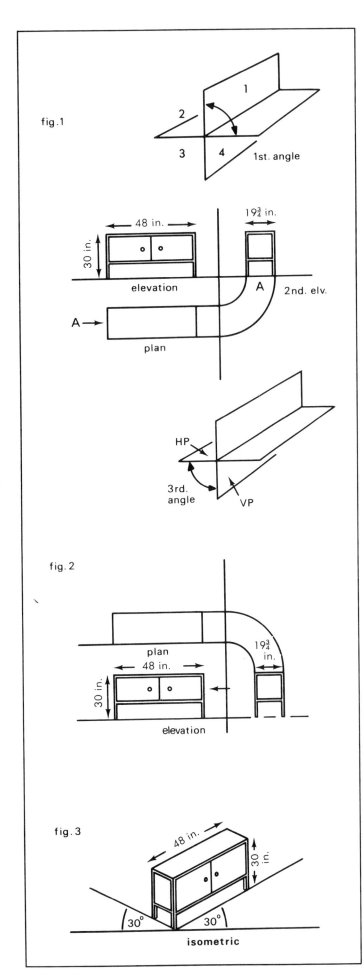

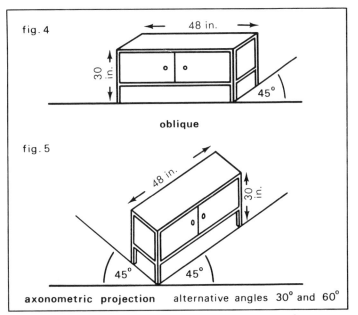

Drawing presentation

The drawings on this page show various methods of projection all of which may be used by the designer-craftsman to illustrate objects. An outline drawing of a framed carcase has been selected to illustrate the different visual qualities of each. All are drawn to the same scale.

Fig. 1 Orthographic projection (first angle)
A method commonly used in this country, it gives concise information in relation to each surface viewed. This form of projection enables an article to be drawn and dimensioned accurately, especially for the purpose of production.

Fig. 2 Orthographic projection (third angle)
Used mainly in the U.S.A., the chief difference between this and first angle projection being the plan which is shown above the elevation, see drawing. Many British designers prefer first angle projection and some practise successfully in a combination of both.

Fig. 3 Isometric projection
This is a pictorial projection based on the use of 30° set square for receding lines, although these angles may be varied to suit particular purposes. Actual dimensions are used with this projection. It also lends itself as a useful base for free-hand sketching. See also isometric projection of desk on page 103.

Fig. 4 Oblique projection
This is a pictorial view produced direct from an actual elevation. The receding lines are usually of 45° but 30° and 60° angles are often used, and these lines are drawn half their actual dimension. A desk illustrated on page 103 is drawn in oblique and isometric projection respectively. It is interesting to compare these two drawings; the dotted lines in the oblique projection show quite clearly the effect of halving the actual side dimension. Although the isometric projection gives a fairly close approximation to the visual appearance, there appears to be less distortion in the oblique projection shown here.

Fig. 5 Axonometric projection
A method used by architects to show details, interiors,.etc. Main advantages are (1) the speed with which it can be drawn, (2) that all right angles in plan are shown in true shape. See axonometric drawings of writing table and chair page 103.

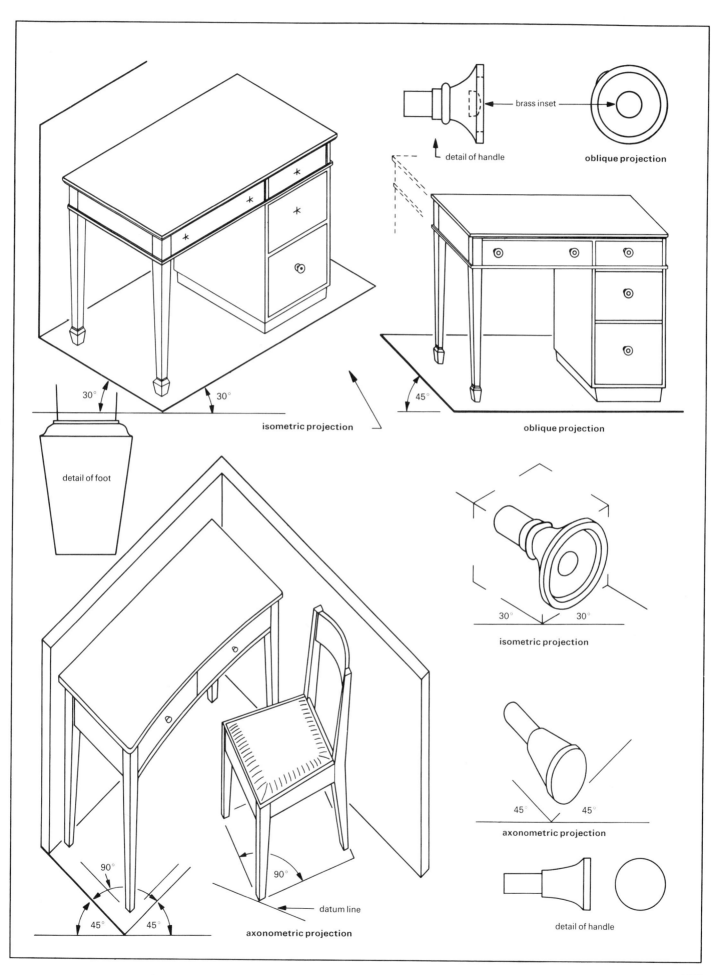

brass inset

detail of handle

oblique projection

oblique projection

30°　　　30°

isometric projection

45°

detail of foot

isometric projection

30°　　30°

axonometric projection

45°　　45°

90°

90°

45°　　45°

datum line

axonometric projection

detail of handle

Designs

A collection of designs for furniture and other articles of woodwork covering some of the requirements of modern living, is included in this section. They comprise the following: tables, chairs, sideboards and storage units, desks and bureaux, wall furniture and bookcases, bedroom furniture and miscellaneous pieces.

These are illustrated with photographs and in some cases line diagrams suggesting sizes for specific purposes. It is hoped that this information based on a wide range and variety will help to stimulate ideas.

The photographs show designs which have been selected to include work from well-known designers. The captions give useful information on a wide variety of materials, specifications, wood and metal finishes, types of handles, fittings and upholstery.

Note: When designing work based on period pieces, information is readily available through museums and libraries. Making measured drawings from actual specimen pieces is a most useful and practical experience for the designer-craftsman.

Tables

The measurements given in the line diagrams are based on the study in recent years of ergonomics and anthropometrics.

To seat four persons comfortably around a table, an allowance of approximately 580mm (23in) should be made for each sitter.

A square table to seat four persons should be about 1,015mm (40in), and a rectangular table 1,520mm (60in) ×760mm (30in) will seat six persons.

Circular tops 1,120mm (44in) diameter seat four and 1,220mm (48in) diameter seat six.

The clearance between underside of table framing and chair should not be less than 150mm (6in).

Above:
Circular fixed top table, 1,220mm (48in) diameter ×710mm (28in). In light beech, solid and veneered.
Designed by: Ray Leigh, A.A.Dip., F.S.I.A.; Trevor Chinn; and Martin Hall, M.S.I.A.
Photograph by courtesy of Gordon Russell.

Opposite left:
Small coffee table in guarea with Formica top.
635mm (2ft 1in) ×405mm (1ft 4in) ×330mm (1ft 1in).
Designed and made by the author.

Opposite right:
Nest of three tables with teak or rosewood veneers.
Largest table, 570mm (1ft 10½in) ×370mm (1ft 2½in) ×520mm (1ft 8½in) high. Danish.
Photograph courtesy of Heal and Son Ltd.

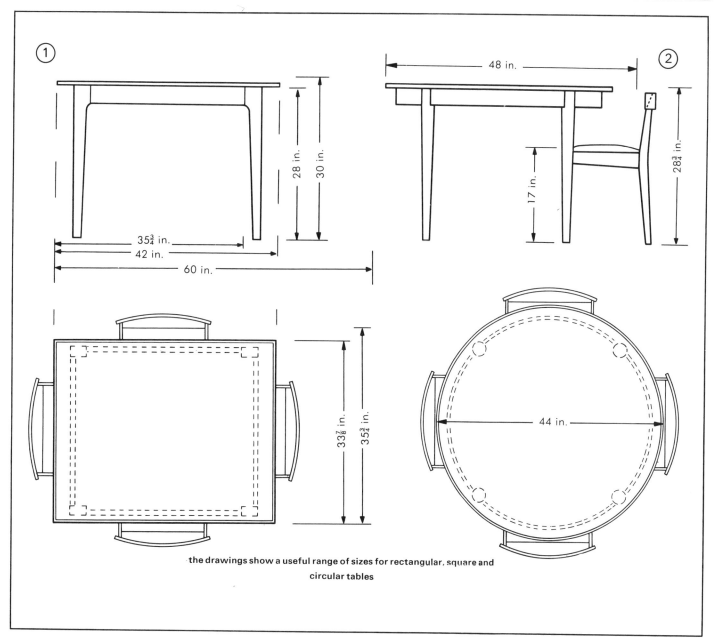

①

28 in.
30 in.
35¾ in.
42 in.
60 in.
33⅞ in.
35¾ in.

②

48 in.
17 in.
28¾ in.
44 in.

the drawings show a useful range of sizes for rectangular, square and circular tables

Left:
Occasional table with drawer, made in teak. A portion of the top is faced with Formica. Note the decorative tenons and wedges. Bowl in teak with rather nicely shaped top edge and base.
Made by a student of Shoreditch College.

Below:
Extending table. 1,220mm/1,830mm (48in/72in) ×760mm (30in) ×710mm (28in).
In afrormosia under frame with teak veneered top. Free standing storage units in teak with contrasting eggshell white finished surfaces, and plinths covered in brown P.V.C. Drawer and door handles are gold anodised aluminium.
Each cabinet is complete in itself, and these can be arranged in a variety of ways.
Designed by: Ray Leigh, A.A.Dip., F.S.I.A.; Trevor Chinn; and Martin Hall, M.S.I.A.
Chairs designed by: R. D. Russell, R.D.I., F.S.I.A.
Photograph by courtesy of Gordon Russell Ltd.

Right:
Coffee table with rosewood veneered top and ebonized underframes, complete with serving tray in rosewood with black plastic. 875mm (2ft 10½in) ×420mm (1ft 4½in) ×480mm (1ft 7in) high.
Designed by: Charles Gage, R.C.A. and made by Heal Furniture Ltd.
Photograph by courtesy of Heal and Son Ltd.

Below:
Dining room suite. Table is veneered in Rio rosewood with solid lipping. Matching sideboard has four doors, interior trays and adjustable shelves. The chairs have loose seats and back cushions. The steel supports are finished in bright chrome.
Designed by: Robin Day, R.D.I., A.R.C.A., F.S.I.A.
Photograph by courtesy of Hille International Ltd.

Left and below:
Circular pillar dining table, 1,190mm (47in) diameter extending with two leaves to 2,390mm (94in). Veneered in teak, Rio rosewood or oak.
Designed by: K. E. Ekselius, and made by Heal Furniture Ltd.
Photograph by courtesy of Heal and Son Ltd.
Table extended.

Bottom right:
Drum dining table in Rio rosewood veneers, 1,420mm (56in) diameter with four drawers. This is an up-to-date version of a traditional English library table, with a combination of 18th century elegance and 20th century simplicity.
Photograph by courtesy of Archie Shine Ltd.

Bottom left:
Pillar dining table, 1,220mm (48in) diameter in Rio rosewood with off-white plastic laminate covered top to match the column.
Designed by: Brian Long, M.S.I.A. and made by Heal Furniture Ltd.
Photograph by courtesy of Heal and Son Ltd.

Right:
Dining table in Columbian pine, made specially for a cottage.
1,295mm (51in) ×710mm (28in) ×740mm (29in).
Designed and made by the author.

Below:
Oval table in rosewood on cast aluminium legs. 2,035mm (80in) ×1,090mm (43in).
Photograph by courtesy of Archie Shine Ltd.

Chairs

Seat widths: See line diagrams dealing with chairs, pages 110 and 111.

A comfortable width is 457mm (18in) and if required for lengthy periods should definitely not be less than 432mm (17in).

Seat height: Approximately 432mm (17in).
A slightly tilted seat base and angled back rest helps comfortable seating in a chair. For shoulder support a height of 510mm (20in) — 635mm (25in) from seat is recommended. To give back and head support as much as 900mm (35½in) may be necessary.

Arm rests: A useful distance between arm rests is 480mm (19in). A workable height for an arm rest is 200mm (8in) and when padded about 215mm (8½in). A minimum and maximum range for arm rests is 190mm (7½in) — 250mm (10in).

Below left:
Dining chair in teak.

Below right:
Carver in teak to match dining chair.
Photographs by courtesy of Heal and Son Ltd.

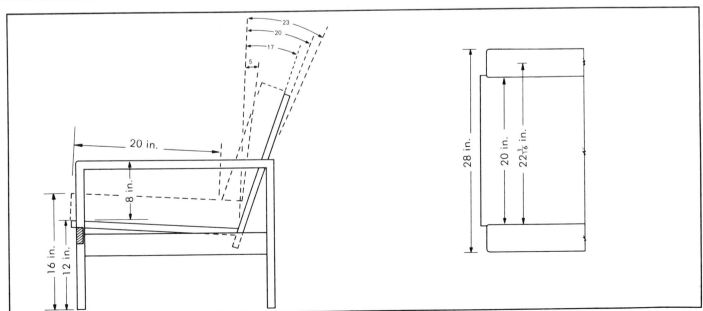

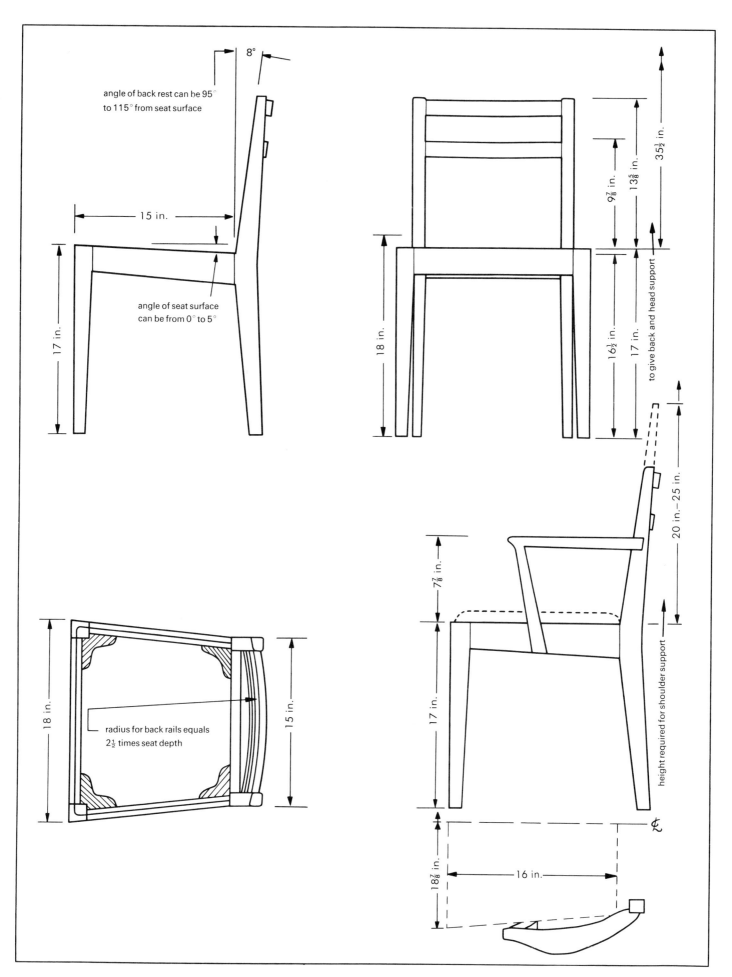

8°

angle of back rest can be 95°
to 115° from seat surface

15 in.

17 in.

angle of seat surface
can be from 0° to 5°

$9\frac{7}{8}$ in.

$13\frac{5}{8}$ in.

$35\frac{1}{2}$ in.

18 in.

$16\frac{1}{2}$ in.

17 in.

to give back and head support

20 in.–25 in.

$7\frac{7}{8}$ in.

17 in.

height required for shoulder support

$18\frac{7}{8}$ in.

16 in.

18 in.

15 in.

radius for back rails equals
$2\frac{1}{2}$ times seat depth

Left:
Table and chairs in cherry wood, leather and cane.
Designed and made by John Makepeace, M.S.I.A.
for the Attlee Memorial Room, Toynbee Hall.

Below:
Dining room suite.
Chairs are upholstered and stackable.
Also shown are storage cabinets and circular table.
Designed by: Ray Leigh, A.A.Dip., F.S.I.A.; Trevor Chinn; and
Martin Hall, M.S.I.A.
Made by Gordon Russell Ltd.
Photograph by courtesy of Gordon Russell Ltd.

Below:
Armchair in teak with turned legs.
Made by a student of Shoreditch College.

Bottom:
Memorial bench seat in teak.
Made by students of Shoreditch College.
Incised lettering by the author.

Right:
Upholstered armchair on a teak base.
Made by a student of Shoreditch College.

E.F.MARSHALL M.A. PRINCIPAL 1954-64

Sideboards

The line diagrams on this page give a range of sideboard sizes suitable either for the small cottage or for the more spacious accommodation of larger houses.

The sideboards illustrated on page 115 show various design features.

The carcase of the sideboard shown in Fig. 1, opposite, projects 230mm (9in) over each end of the stool or stand. It has sliding doors with sunk pulls, and the drawer fronts are flush and also made with sunk pulls. Note the small sinking arranged to break the line of the top — see constructional details page 86.

The sideboard, Fig. 2, has a carcase and stool of the same length; the rebate worked on the top edge of the stool makes an attractive design feature. The doors and drawers are shown flush, and the handles are to be made of aluminium and brushed finished.

Fig. 3 shows a sideboard with an interesting framed stool, and tambour doors.

Sideboard veneered in Rio rosewood, with oak-lined interior, generously fitted with shelves and removable trays.
2,235mm (7ft 4in) ×420mm (1ft 4½in) ×950mm (3ft 1½in) high.
Danish.
Designed by: H. Rosengren Hansen.
Photograph by courtesy of Heal and Son Ltd.

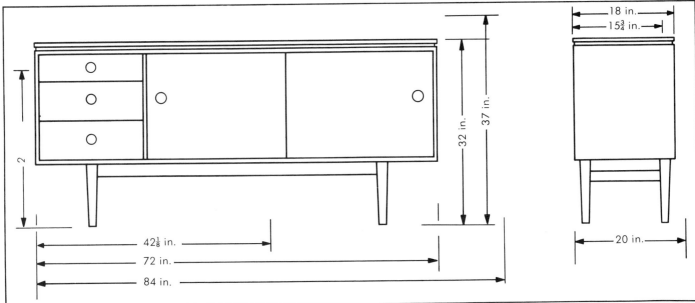

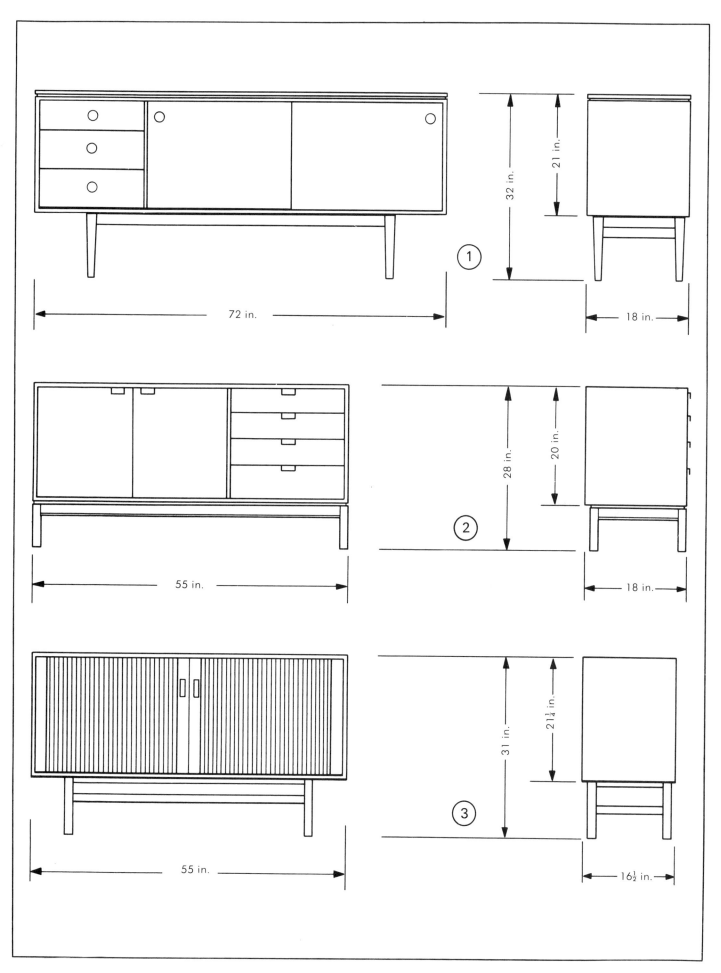

72 in.

32 in.

21 in.

18 in.

①

55 in.

28 in.

20 in.

18 in.

②

55 in.

31 in.

$21\frac{1}{4}$ in.

$16\frac{1}{2}$ in.

③

Left:
Cabinet on stand with drawer. Made of English oak, the doors are embellished with linenfold panels.
Made by a student of Shoreditch College.

Below:
Room dividers.
Right: in teak and Brazilian rosewood, with stainless steel rods to support top shelving.
Left: in teak with sliding doors and sunk handles. The top cabinet is fitted with sliding glass doors. The lower and top carcases are suspended between two shaped frames, the raised pellets giving a decorative treatment
Made by students of Shoreditch College.

Bottom:
Sideboard in teak. Designed to be used without the stand or underframe if required as a wall unit. Note flush drop handles on drawer fronts. Length 2,135mm (7ft) depth 455mm (1ft 6in) height 760mm (2ft 6in).
Photograph by courtesy of Archie Shine Ltd.

Below:
Storage assembly in teak, solid and veneer. Low storage units are 915mm (3ft) ×495mm (1ft 7½in) ×730mm (2ft 4¾in) high, each contains a sliding tray. Open bookshelves or bookcase/ display cabinets fitted with sliding glass doors are 915mm (3ft) ×260mm (10¼in) ×870mm (2ft 10¼in) high.
Designed by: Robert Heritage, R.D.I., Des. R.C.A., F.S.I.A. and made by Gordon Russell. Photograph by Gordon Russell Ltd.

Right:
1,370mm (4ft 6in) free standing wall storage unit in Rio rosewood veneers, consisting of three separate carcases. It has deep storage in the base unit, and accommodation for writing or drinks in fall front carcase. There is generous cupboard space in the top carcase. The bottom carcase is 610mm (2ft) deep overall. Photograph by courtesy of Archie Shine Ltd.

Bottom:
Sideboard in teak, with two deep drawers and cupboard space. The doors are made with sunk pulls; the drawer pulls are an integral part of the drawers and are worked on the solid. Made by a student of Shoreditch College.

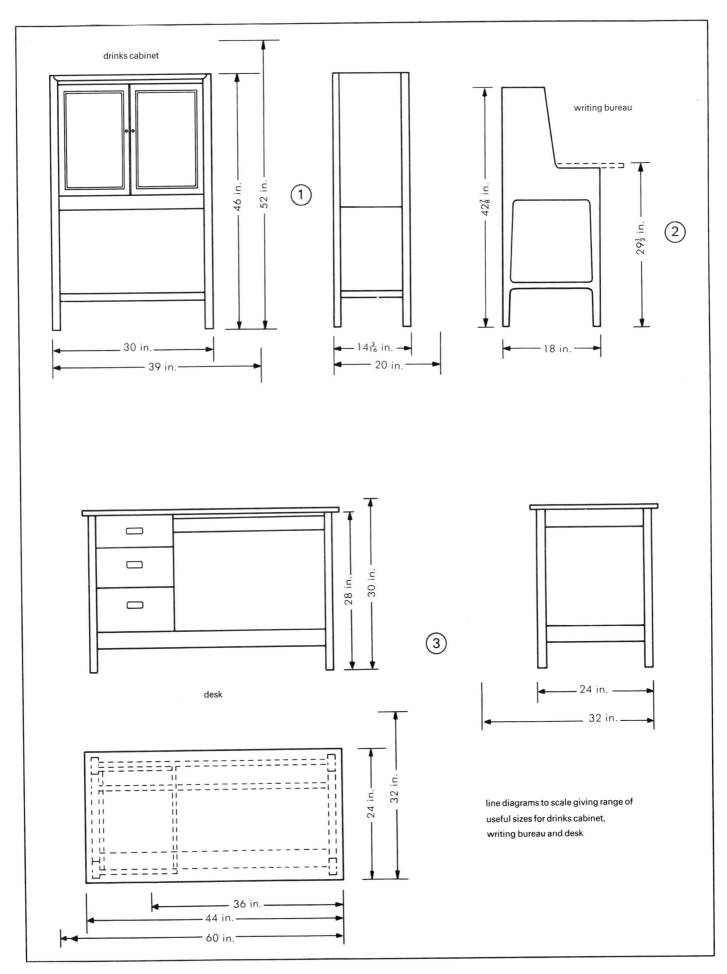

drinks cabinet

46 in.

52 in.

①

$14\frac{3}{16}$ in.

20 in.

30 in.

39 in.

writing bureau

$42\frac{7}{8}$ in.

$29\frac{1}{2}$ in.

②

18 in.

desk

③

28 in.

30 in.

24 in.

32 in.

32 in.

24 in.

36 in.

44 in.

60 in.

line diagrams to scale giving range of
useful sizes for drinks cabinet,
writing bureau and desk

Right:
Office furniture, veneered in teak.
Frames are square section steel, black epoxy powder coated or bright chrome finished anodised aluminium.
Designed by: Robin Day, R.D.I., A.R.C.A., F.S.I.A.
Photograph by courtesy of Hille International Ltd.

Below:
A spacious desk with overhang that enables it to be used as a conference table. Pedestals and the front portion of this desk are veneered in Rio rosewood, and the writing surface is covered in hide. Legs and framing members are of square section steel chrome finish, or black epoxy powder coated.
Width 1,830mm (6ft) ×depth 915mm (3ft) ×height 730mm (2ft 4¾in).
Designed by: Robin Day, R.D.I., A.R.C.A., F.S.I.A.
Photograph by courtesy of Hille International Ltd.

Bottom:
Leather bound desk and storage units. 2,000mm (6ft 6¾in) × 750mm (2ft 5½in). Made by John Makepeace, M.S.I.A.
Photograph by courtesy of John Makepeace.

Left:
Desk veneered in Rio rosewood, with rectangular steel legs, bright chrome finish. Double pedestal. 1,980mm (6ft 6in) × 915mm (3ft) ×740mm (2ft 5in).
Designed by: Robin Day, R.D.I., A.R.C.A., F.S.I.A.
Photograph by courtesy of Hille International Ltd.

Below left:
Bureau/bookcase with teak veneer.
With three drawers and sliding top. Above the sliding top are three small drawers and pigeon holes, all enclosed by tambour shutters. 1,000mm (3ft 3½in) wide ×1,800mm (5ft 11in) high ×430mm (1ft 4¾in) deep. Danish.
Photograph by courtesy of Heal and Son Ltd.
For wall bureau with drawers and stationery units, see photograph, page 81.

Below right:
Unit cupboards and bookcases in utile.
The cupboard doors are lipped with yew and the handles are also in yew. These units can be arranged in a variety of interesting ways.
These pieces were designed and made by the author. 1950.

Rostrum office by John Makepeace, M.S.I.A.
Bird's eye view, showing the ample space for working, storage and filing, etc.
Photograph by courtesy of John Makepeace.

Rostrum office by John Makepeace, M.S.I.A.
Overall diameter, 2,000mm (6ft 6¾in).
Rostrum is covered in brown felt. Pillars in purple polish, with sycamore, cream vinyl and acrylic adjustable shelves.
Photograph by courtesy of John Makepeace.

Bedroom furniture

Wardrobe sizes vary considerably according to needs; those suggested in the line diagrams, Fig. 1 page 123, are suitable for a good range of domestic requirements. Suggested sizes for other bedroom furniture is also given.

Fig. 2 shows dressing tables.

Fig. 3 shows small dressing table.

Fig. 4 shows dressing stool.

Fig. 5 shows chest of three deep drawers.

Bed sizes

Bunk or child's size: 760mm (2ft 6in)
Single: 915mm (3ft) or 1,065mm (3ft 6in)
Double beds should not be less than 1,220mm (4ft); the 1,370mm (4ft 6in) and 1,520mm (5ft) sizes are preferable. Lengths are usually, 1,905mm (6ft 3in) and

1980mm (6ft 6in). Height of bed: 510mm (1ft 8in) to top of mattress is a comfortable height for making up a bed, although the divan types are usually made lower.

Below:
Photographs show a bedroom system based on a 100mm (4in) module, with afrormosia veneers. The basic components are all 560mm (1ft 10in) deep.
Designed by: Dennis Bull, M.S.I.A.
Photograph by courtesy of Heal and Son Ltd.

Left:
Cheval mirror, made in English yew and sycamore. Made by a student of Shoreditch College.

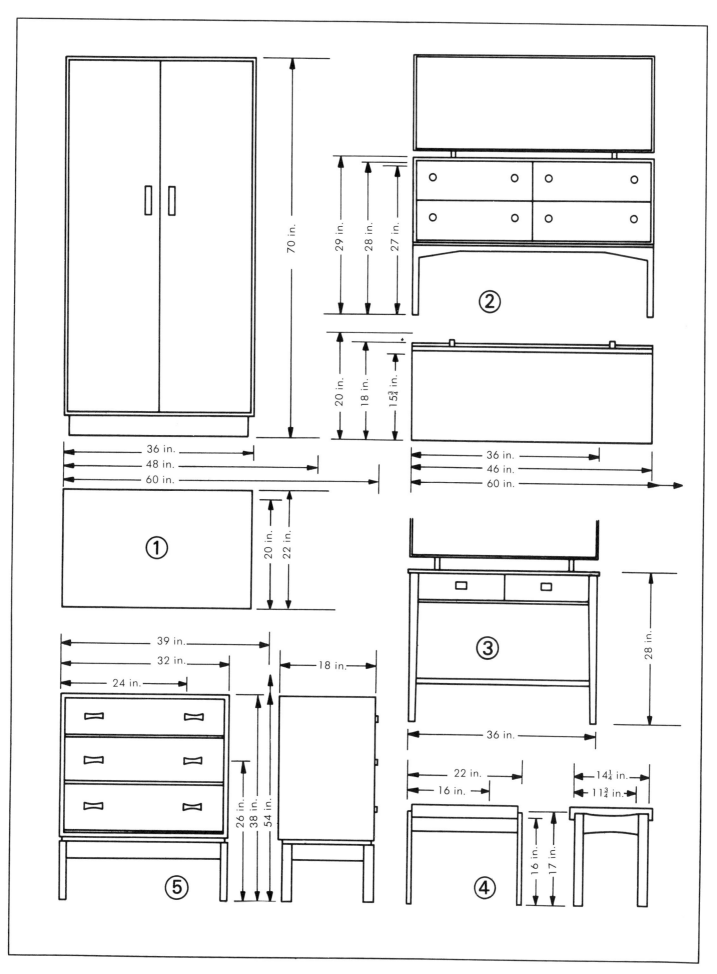

70 in.

29 in.
28 in.
27 in.

20 in.
18 in.
15¾ in.

②

36 in.
48 in.
60 in.

36 in.
46 in.
60 in.

①

20 in.
22 in.

28 in.

③

39 in.
32 in.
24 in.

18 in.

36 in.

26 in.
38 in.
54 in.

22 in.
16 in.

14¼ in.
11¾ in.

16 in.
17 in.

⑤

④

Right:
The bedroom/study. Dressing table assembly consists of two three-drawer chests, 635mm (2ft 1in) ×755mm (2ft 5¾in) with a link shelf 800mm (2ft 7½in).
Arm chair is upholstered. Occasional table in light beech, solid and veneer 760mm (2ft 6in) ×760mm (2ft 6in) ×355mm (1ft 2in). Underbed storage box, 1,780mm (5ft 10in) ×610mm (2ft) ×195mm (7¾in), moves freely on rollers.
Bed 2,000mm (6ft 6¾in) ×980mm (3ft 2½in) ×320mm (12½in) to spring base.
Designed by: Ray Leigh, A.A.Dip., F.S.I.A.; Trevor Chinn; and Martin Hall, M.S.I.A.
Photograph by courtesy of Gordon Russell.

Below:
The Hille storage wall system.
Designed by: Alan Turville, M.S.I.A. on a 10cm (4in) module. The units are all wall-mounted, and are made of veneered high density particle board, with solid wood lipped edges. Made in a range of veneers, finished catalytic melamine lacquer.
Photograph by courtesy of Hille International Ltd.

Other design areas

The designs in the following pages suggest various areas of work which the artist-craftsman might find stimulating and rewarding. They include:

1 Laminated and steam bent wood, formed plywood work
The technique of laminating eliminates short grain and offers unique design possibilities for shaped work. It is also economical.

The sketches on pages 125 and 126 show various techniques for splicing solid timber and plywood.

Below:
Three-legged table in oak with laminated beech rails. Top can be of plate glass or veneered and lipped laminboard. Designed and made by the author.

Bottom:
Reclining chair with framing of solid and laminated ash. Made by a student at Shoreditch College.

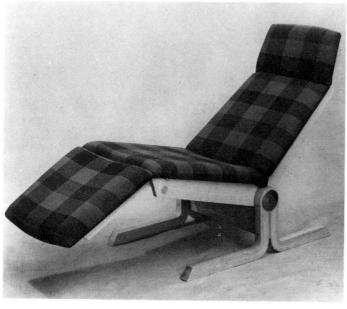

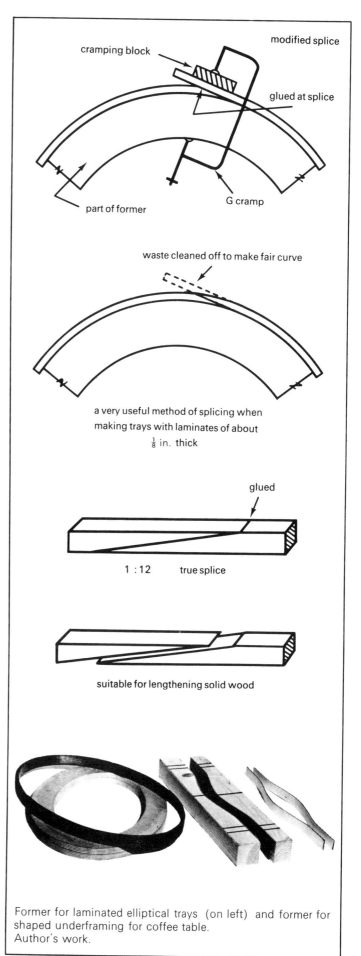

Former for laminated elliptical trays (on left) and former for shaped underframing for coffee table.
Author's work.

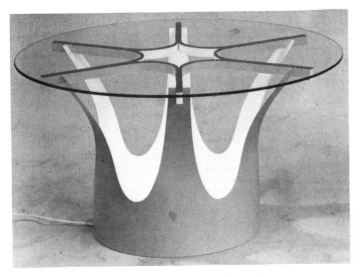

Table with plate glass top, and laminated top framing, supported by a formed plywood base. Enamelled finish. Made by a student of Shoreditch College.

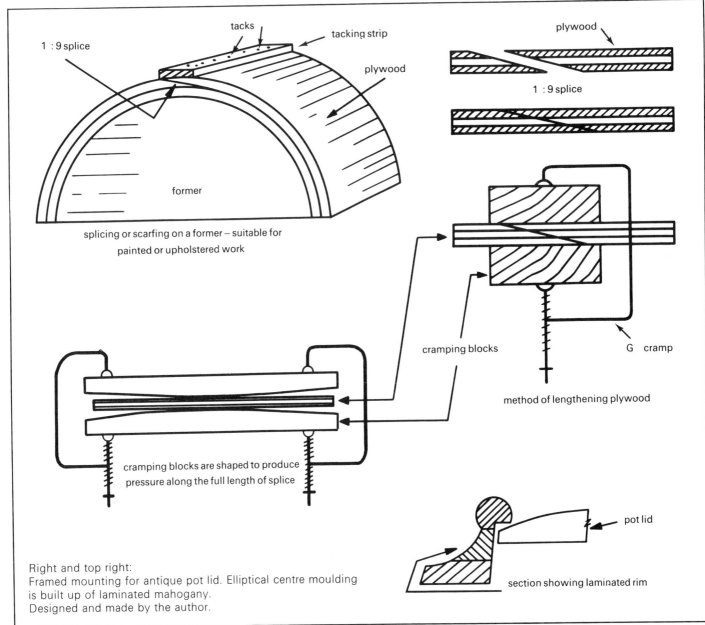

tacks

tacking strip

1 : 9 splice

plywood

plywood

1 : 9 splice

former

splicing or scarfing on a former – suitable for painted or upholstered work

cramping blocks

G cramp

method of lengthening plywood

cramping blocks are shaped to produce pressure along the full length of splice

pot lid

section showing laminated rim

Right and top right:
Framed mounting for antique pot lid. Elliptical centre moulding is built up of laminated mahogany.
Designed and made by the author.

2 Church furniture

Offers opportunity for good design and craftsmanship in both traditional and modern tastes.

Below:
Gluing up of altar rail. After fitting, all parts were finally cleaned up and polished, before gluing up. The turned balusters are scribed over the rounded top surface of the bottom rail. The altar rail was made for Egham Parish Church, Surrey by students of Shoreditch College.

Right:
A fully adjustable music stand, in English oak. Designed and made by the author.

Bottom:
Two chairs in English oak.

Altar table in English oak.
All four pieces designed and made by the author.

3 Sculpture and carving, incised lettering, inlay and turned work

Working in wood encompasses an enormous range and variety of techniques. This gives the keen craftsman an opportunity to express his individuality according to his experience and ability.

Right:
Chess trophy in mahogany and rosewood.
Sycamore and rosewood inlay, 255mm (10in) high.
Designed and made by the author.

Below left:
'Hare': in Brazilian walnut, mounted with a stainless steel rod on to a rosewood base.
Made by a student of Shoreditch College.

Below right:
Large bowl fitted with turntable, and set of small bowls, all in lime. Spoons are in laminated rosewood and shaped.
Made by a student of Shoreditch College.

Bottom:
'Alana' Name and number plate in oak. Author's work.